career advancement for
women in the federal service

public affairs and administration
(editor: James S. Bowman)
vol. 28

Garland reference library
of social science
vol. 867

the public affairs and administration series:
James S. Bowman, editor

1. career planning, development, and management: an annotated bibliography
   Jonathan P. West
2. professional dissent: an annotated bibliography and resource guide
   James S. Bowman, Frederick A. Elliston, Paula Lockhart
3. American public administration: a bibliographical guide to the literature
   Gerald E. Caiden, Richard A. Loverd, Thomas J. Pavlek, Lynn F. Sipe, Molly M. Wong
4. public administration in rural areas and small jurisdictions: a guide to the literature
   Beth Walter Honadle
5. comparative public administration: an annotated bibliography
   Mark W. Huddleston
6. the bureaucratic state: an annotated bibliography
   Robert D. Miewald
7. labor management relations in the public sector: an annotated bibliography
   N. Joseph Cayer, Sherry S. Dickerson
8. public choice theory in public administration: an annotated bibliography
   Nicholas F. Lovrich, Max Neiman
9. public policy analysis: an annotated bibliography
   John S. Robey
10. public personnel administration: an annotated bibliography
    Sarah Y. Bowman, Jay M. Shafritz
11. news media and public policy: an annotated bibliography
    Joseph P. McKerns
12. equal employment opportunity and affirmative action: a sourcebook
    Floyd D. Weatherspoon
13. voluntary associations: an annotated bibliography
    Donato J. Pugliese
14. administration and development in the Arab world: an annotated bibliography
    Jamil E. Jreisat, Zaki R. Ghosheh
15. organization behavior in American public administration: an annotated bibliography
    Aurora T. Payad
16. pay inequity: a guide to research on social influences
    Eliot R. Hammer
17. program evaluation: an annotated bibliography
    Patrick S. Dynes, Mary K. Marvel
18. civil service reform: an annotated bibliography
    David L. Dillman
19. gubernatorial and presidential transitions: an annotated bibliography and resource guide
    James S. Bowman, Ronald L. Monet
20. ethics and public policy: an annotated bibliography
    Peter J. Bergerson
21. public sector productivity: a resource guide
    Marc Holzer, Arie Halachmi
22. delivering government services: an annotated bibliography
    William F. Murin, Judith Pryor
23. employee assistance programs: an annotated bibliography
    Donna R. Kemp
24. public opinion polls and survey research: a selective annotated bibliography of U.S. guides and studies from the 1980s
    Graham R. S. Walden
25. public budgeting and financial management: an annotated bibliography
    Jack Rabin, Ernest C. Cerino, Jr., Maria Eugenia Dimas, Deborah Lowden Donahue
26. public administration research guide
    Virginia R. Cherry, Marc Holzer
27. political corruption: scope and resources
    Elaine R. Johansen
28. career advancement for women in the federal service: an annotated bibliography and resource book
    Lynn C. Ross

career advancement for
women in the federal service:
*an annotated bibliography
and resource book*

Lynn C. Ross

Garland Publishing, Inc. • New York & London
1993

© 1993 Lynn C. Ross
All rights reserved

Library of Congress Cataloging-in-Publication Data

Ross, Lynn C.
　　Career advancement for women in the federal service : an annotated bibliography and resource book / by Lynn C. Ross.
　　　　p.　cm. — (Public affairs and administration ; vol. 28) (Garland reference library of social science ; vol. 867)
　　ISBN 0-8153-1058-7 (alk. paper)
　　1. Women in the civil service—United States—Bibliography.
2. Career development—United States—Bibliography.　I. Title.
II. Series: Public affairs and administration ; 28.　III. Series: Garland reference library of social science ; v. 867.
Z7164.C6R67　　1993
[JK721]
016.353001'082—dc20　　　　　　　　　　　　　93-19100
　　　　　　　　　　　　　　　　　　　　　　　　　　CIP

Printed on acid-free, 250-year-life paper
Manufactured in the United States of America

For My Parents, Dave and Sue Ann Ross,
who taught me the value of public service.

Contents

SERIES FOREWORD ix

FOREWORD xi

ACKNOWLEDGMENTS xiv

INTRODUCTION xvi

CHAPTER 1: ADVANCING CAREERS
    Planning & Strategies 3
    Management Style 19
    Workforce Changes 26

CHAPTER 2: BARRIERS TO ADVANCEMENT
    The "Glass Ceiling" and Other Impediments 31
    Sex Segregation 46
    Stereotypes 48

CHAPTER 3: AFFIRMATIVE ACTION & EQUAL
              EMPLOYMENT OPPORTUNITY
    General 51
    Representation of Women in the Workforce 60
    Women and Recruitment 69
    Women and Promotions 71
    Discrimination Based on Sex 74

    Resources 82

CHAPTER 4: SEXUAL HARASSMENT
    The Issues & the Prevention 91
    Relevant Laws and Regulations 104
    Resources 109

CHAPTER 5: PAY EQUITY
    The Research & the Debate 111
    Resources 125

CHAPTER 6: MENTORS & NETWORKING
    The Pros & Cons of Having Connections 129
    Associations & Unions 139

CHAPTER 7: WOMEN & MEN
    Similarities & Differences 153
    Communication Between Women and Men 164

CHAPTER 8: TRAINING
    General 167
    Federal Training Resources 174

CHAPTER 9: WOMEN IN NON-TRADITIONAL
                  OCCUPATIONS 185

CHAPTER 10: WORK & FAMILY ISSUES
    General Issues 195
    Child Care and Other Benefits 202
    Flexible Work Arrangements 205
    Multiple Roles & Competing Demands 212
    Resources 217

CHAPTER 11: BIBLIOGRAPHIES & OTHER GENERAL
                  RESOURCES
    Pertinent Bibliographies 227
    General Resources 232
    Merit System Principles 237
    Prohibited Personnel Practices 239
    Landmarks for Women in the Federal Service 241

INDEX 243

Series Foreword

The twentieth century has seen public administration come of age as a field of study and practice. As a result of the dramatic growth in government, and the accompanying information explosion, many individuals—managers, academicians and their students, researchers—in organizations feel that they do not have ready access to important information. In an increasingly complex world, more and more people need published material to help solve problems.

The scope of the field and the lack of a comprehensive information system has frustrated users, disseminators, and generators of knowledge in public administration. While there have been some initiatives in recent years, the documentation and control of the literature have been generally neglected. Indeed, major gaps in the development of the literature, the bibliographic structure of the discipline, have evolved.

Garland Publishing, Inc., inaugurated this series as an authoritative guide to information sources in public administration. It seeks to consolidate the gains made in the growth and maturation of the profession.

The Series consists of three tiers:
1. core volumes keyed to the major subfields in public administration, such as personnel management, public budgeting, and organizational behavior;
2. bibliographies focusing on substantive areas of administration; and

3. titles on topical issues in the profession, such as civil service, reform, productivity, and ethics.

Each book will be compiled by one or more specialists in the area. The authors—practitioners and scholars—are selected in open competition from across the country. They design their work to include an introductory essay, a wide variety of bibliographic materials, and, where appropriate, an information resource section. Thus each contribution in the collection provides a systematic basis for managers and researchers to make informed judgments in the course of their work.

Since no single volume can adequately encompass such a broad, interdisciplinary subject, the Series has been a continuous project incorporating new bodies of literature as needed. Its titles represent the initial building blocks in an operating information system for public affairs and administration. It is hoped that not only will the Series serve to summarize knowledge in the field but also will contribute to its advancement.

This collection of book-length bibliographies is the product of considerable collaboration on the part of many people. Special appreciation is extended to the editors and staff of Garland Publishing, Inc., to the individual contributors in the Public Affairs and Administration Series, and to the anonymous reviewers of each of the volumes. Inquiries should be made to the Series Editor.

James S. Bowman
School of Public Administration and Policy
Florida State University

Foreword

The year 2000 is now just a few short years away. Will this nation's civil service system be ready for the challenges of the twenty-first century? The answer is "no" if all of the nation's human resources are not properly involved. The federal government has been better than most employers in providing itself with an equal opportunity to benefit from the skills and abilities of all. But there are "miles to go before we sleep." As has been noted in the Introduction of the extraordinary annotated bibliography: "Women represent more than half of the federal workforce, but they encumber just over 10 percent of the senior executive positions and only about 14 percent of the middle management jobs."

Noting that almost two-thirds of the new entrants into the general workforce between now and the year 2000 will be women is important. This means there will need to be greater consideration of all of the issues affecting women in the workforce. There must be a determination of the barriers to achievement; an understanding of affirmative action and equal employment opportunity. Guidance must be given to women on career planning and the manner in which they must work with their fellow MEN. And importantly there must be an emphasis on the development of strategies for the proper balancing of work and family. Changes will have to be made with regard to child care and other benefits as well as flexible work arrangements. *Career Advancement for Women in the Federal Service: An Annotated Bibliography and Resource Book* provides an outstanding range of annotations to the literature that can help everyone plan and prepare for the role of women in the federal workforce for now and in the future.

This comprehensive annotation will be a valuable tool for practitioners, researchers and individuals concerned about their careers. I wish that *Career Advancement for Women in the Federal Service* had been available to me at several key points in my career. This book has it all! Had this annotation been available when I began my career as a clerk-typist after earning a law degree, the section "Representation of Women in the Workforce" would have been useful. There one can find the annotations of important literature on employment trends in the federal government. This could have prompted me to start my job search in agencies with the best record for the employment of women.

The bibliography is especially useful for practitioners. For those in the human resource management professions there are serviceable annotations on women and recruitment; women and promotions; and federal training resources. With regard to training, for example, one could be led to articles on effective executive training programs for women in Canada; on skills needed for women at the top; and on the future of federal training. Furthermore, the annotation provides excellent information on the elements and participation qualifications of existing training programs available to women.

Lynn Ross's bibliography is most useful on a variety of issues affecting women in the military. Among the chapters that are relevant to those addressing the various problems of women in the military is, "Barriers to Advancement" which annotates the *Fortune* article on why women are not getting to the top. Also noted is the intriguing annotation of the article on "Advancement by Women in Hierarchical Organizations: A Multilevel Analysis of Problems and Prospects" in the *Journal of Applied Behavioral Science*. The military has had to address the problem of sexual harassment. It will be helpful to the work of the Defense Advisory Committee and others to have ready access to the current literature cited in the chapter on "Sexual Harassment."

In 1986, I wrote *The Uniform Guidelines on Employee Selection Procedures: A Background Report*. Days and days of research would have been reduced had I had available the Ross chapter on "Affirmative Action and Equal Employment Opportunity."

As Director of the U.S. Office of Personnel Management, I was responsible for ensuring that the agency address each topic covered in the chapters of this annotation. Issues had to be explored. Decisions had to be made. Speeches had to be given. For policymakers and program directors in the federal government, I say: "Start with *Career Advancement for Women in the Federal Service: An Annotated Bibliography and Resource Book*." I wish I had had it available to me. For all interested in human resource management, I say: "Have this excellent comprehensive bibliography on the shelf next to your dictionary and thesaurus."

Constance Berry Newman

Acknowledgments

One of the many wonderful discoveries I made while conducting searches for this bibliography is that Librarians are some of the most dedicated and knowledgeable "public servants" around. Special thanks to Catherine Tashjean at the U.S. Office of Personnel Management (OPM) who gave me lots of valuable advice, and generously pulled many sources for me from her Library's collection. Leon Brody at OPM also quickly and cheerfully helped me dig up information. Colleen Allen at the Department of Labor spent several hours giving guidance and advice that proved very valuable, and Sheridan Harvey at the Library of Congress lent her expertise and experience to the project.

I also owe a debt of gratitude to the many women, too numerous to name, at the many women's organizations I contacted. They gave me insights into issues that are important to women in the workplace. Lynn Eppard at Federally Employed Women, Inc., was especially helpful. Kathy Naff at the Merit Systems Protection Board got me involved in another project which led to the opportunity to do this book; she also gave me some wonderful sources. Les Bodian, Kelly Ross Kantz and Greg Zygiel generously donated time and talent to this project, and Sylvia White, a dear friend and colleague, graciously helped with typing. Special thanks also to Rick Lowe who lent his time and support at the final stages of the book.

I am indebted to Dr. Pat Ingraham and Donna Beecher for their advocacy on this effort, and in general. And Dr. James Bowman, series editor, who asked me to do this project was a wonderfully patient guide through the entire exercise. I also feel it necessary to acknowledge the women and men in the federal civil service with whom I work every day. They are a perennial source of wisdom, inspiration, and challenge. As a result of their examples, my commitment to public service continues to grow.

Finally, and most of all, thanks to my wonderful husband, Jon Bazemore, who always seems to find the energy to support me personally and professionally--I suppose I could have finished this project without him, but it would have been so much more painful!

Introduction

Women in any workforce, public or private, confront the same choices that men face related to managing their careers--picking an occupational specialty, committing to a particular organization, participating in developmental activities, and so on. Yet women also frequently encounter different challenges--structural and organizational discrimination, disproportionate responsibility for children and family, inequitable pay, negative stereotyping, et cetera. And women who aspire to reach the management ranks in any organization must deal with the complexities, subtleties, and even the good or bad fortune related to managing a career.

In order to fully understand these issues, it is necessary to briefly examine the history as well as the culture and system in which women in the federal civil service currently work. The discussion below begins with an introduction to "representative bureaucracy," the first theory to set forth the notion that different sectors of the population at large must be represented in government in order for government to be representative. Representative bureaucracy is briefly outlined to set the context and provide a framework for what follows. A translation of the theory into the practice is then given, specifically vis-a-vis the history of representation of women in the federal workforce.

Next, barriers to be overcome by women who aspire to succeed in the workplace are discussed. The "Glass Ceiling" phenomenon is presented and defined, and structural and organizational impediments are outlined. The literature tends to describe structural barriers as systemic problems (e.g., occupational segregation, biased job evaluation, pay inequity);

Introduction

organizational barriers, on the other hand, are defined in terms of less formalized assumptions and stereotypes about women that stem from cultural or societal mores. These barriers are highlighted below followed by a short discussion of structural hurdles specific to the civil service.

In the literature, some attribute women's lack of advancement to sex discrimination. A short discussion of the policies and programs designed to combat sex discrimination in the workplace is included. Sexual harassment is also introduced under the rubric of sex discrimination and is included later as a separate chapter.

Despite the pitfalls and problems that are discussed below, there are women who attain high-level positions in the civil service. How they succeed as well as how they manage once they reach the· top is highlighted in "Women Reaching for the Top." Finally, some predictions for the future success of women are made based on an empirical study as well as other forecasts and lessons taken from the whole body of literature.

A REPRESENTATIVE BUREAUCRACY: THE THEORY

In principle, some argue that the public service should be representative of the society for which it labors. If government does the work that enhances the quality of life of her citizens, all points of view should be solicited in the definition and implementation of that pursuit. The assertion that there should be a "representative bureaucracy" dates back to Thomas Jefferson who developed the concept of partisan representation in the early years of the Executive branch. Jefferson felt that the composition of the civil service should broadly reflect the partisan balance of the electorate (see #141). Andrew Jackson expanded this concept to include representation by social class, asserting that public office should be accessible to the rich as well as the poor, "the farmer and the printer."

J. Donald Kingsley, writing about the British civil service in the 1940's took the theory of representative bureaucracy one step further (see #138).

He argued that representation of all groups, not just all classes, was imperative. He wrote,

> The democratic state cannot afford to exclude any considerable body of its citizens from full participation in its affairs. It requires at every point that superior insight and wisdom which is the peculiar product of pooling the diverse streams of experience. In this lies the strength of representative government. Upon it depends the superiority of the democratic civil service over its totalitarian rivals.

Others have argued that the very legitimacy of democratic government is at stake vis-a-vis a representative civil service. Krislov and Rosenbloom (#141) said that "... legitimization is generally conveyed through governmental representation of the public (that is, government of the people) and by public participation in government (government by the people)."

The success, failure, and even the good faith effort of the civil service in becoming a demographically representative entity of the citizenry continues to be debated. Some research argues that it has failed in creating a representative workforce, and that indeed, the system has not been designed to achieve societal representation (see #139); others challenge the basic theory of representative bureaucracy (see #144).

A REPRESENTATIVE BUREAUCRACY: THE PRACTICE

Representation of women in the civil service has waxed and waned over the last two centuries. The number of female employees has usually burgeoned as part of war efforts and shrunk in reaction to economic depressions. Today women occupy about 52 percent of the positions in the federal government.

Introduction xix

In fact, the government was one of the first to "experiment" with bringing relatively large numbers of women into the workforce during the period following the Civil War. This proved to have a profound impact on the American economy, and perhaps an even more profound impact on the status of women in society (see #158).

Over the century that followed the Civil War women continued to serve their country, mostly as clerks. The Civil Service Act of 1883 allowed women to compete for jobs by taking examinations, and the Classification Act of 1923 codified the principle of "equal pay for equal work." Women were making strides.

Relatively significant changes did not come, however, until the President's Commission on the Status of Women (#147) was established in 1961 by John F. Kennedy. Headed by Eleanor Roosevelt, the Commission was charged with studying federal personnel practices related to their effects on the employment of women.

Among other things, the President's Commission discovered that there was a policy based on an 1870 law which allowed agency heads to appoint women to higher-level clerkships "at their discretion." Translated into practice, the law permitted appointing officials to exclude women from consideration for jobs by requesting lists of "eligibles" only from the male population of candidates. Thus, agencies tended to hire and promote men to higher-level positions and women were only considered for lower-level jobs. This practice continued for ninety-two years until, in 1962, Attorney General Robert F. Kennedy declared the 1870 law invalid and Congress subsequently repealed it.

When Lyndon Johnson became President he carried on the work that had previously been started. He surmised based on the Commission's report that the problem was a lack of women in the "pipeline." In response, Johnson established a "recruiting team" to bring more women into the civil service and promote them more quickly than they had been in the past. This team appointed 120 women to top positions and during 1964 and 1965, 3,500 women in the government held positions at a salary of $10,600 or more. Similarly, on the recommendation of the Commission, more flexible and innovative work arrangements were designed in recognition of the disproportionate responsibility women bore for their families.

Indeed representation of women in the workforce has grown significantly since the birth of the bureaucracy, but examination in its most literal sense (i.e., number of employees) may not accurately reflect a representative bureaucracy as defined by the original theorists. The research tends to focus on representation relative to level of influence (i.e., higher ranks in the organization). This suggests that representation in the workforce is not as meaningful if particular groups tend to be doing the low-level, low-status, and typically low-paid work of the organization. Further, if a relatively homogeneous group is in the position to dictate most of the government's policies, then representation is not real. Thus, *managerial* representation may be the truer symbol of women's greater societal representation in decision-making processes.

Although women currently represent more than half of the federal workforce, they incumber just over 10% of the Senior Executive positions, and only about 14% of middle management jobs (GM-13 to GM-15) (U.S. Office of Personnel Management's Central Personnel Data File, 1992). Women are less apt to be promoted than their male counterparts with the same education and experience, yet they tend to receive higher performance ratings (see #117). And although some data show that representation is improving, it seems to be at a relatively slow pace (see #168). All these data beg a very important question--What factors make it more difficult for women to advance?

BARRIERS TO BE OVERCOME

Several variables have been examined by many researchers and practitioners in the public and private sectors related to the progress of women in the workforce and their prospects for future success. Some of the most interesting have to do with the unique, and often elusive impediments that women face in the workforce.

Introduction

Secretary of Labor Lynn Martin, in her Department's Study, outlined some of the barriers women face in employment (although her concentration was the private sector), and highlighted a phenomenon called the "Glass Ceiling" (#101). She said the glass ceiling consists of,

> "...those artificial barriers based on attitudinal or organizational bias that prevent qualified individuals from advancing upward in their organization into management-level positions."

An apt metaphor, the glass ceiling is a transparent obstacle, through which women can see their ultimate goal--the top of the organization--but they don't have the power to shatter it. Barriers can be blatant and overt like structural or organizational systems (e.g., sex segregation) that prevent women from advancing (see, for example, #122), or they can be subtle and intangible (e.g., negative stereotyping), and therefore harder to combat (see, for example, #124).

Some barriers to career advancement may arise even before a woman enters an organization. Societal factors which help mold the decisions that prospective employees make about what occupations to pursue can be viewed as barriers (see #334). Some research shows that women are constrained in their career decisions by psychological barriers related to what they think they are capable of accomplishing, or by fear of success (Horner, 1968). Other social barriers relate to the traditional model under which girls are raised. Traditional sex-role differences support the notion that girls are taught to be care-givers and affiliators, while boys are taught to be more assertive leaders. When transferred to the organizational context, these stereotypes can have a profound effect on perceptions of women's effectiveness and success (see, for example, #128).

Some less concrete, yet often very palpable barriers are assumptions that organizations make about women because they are women. These can include stereotypes that women are not as committed to their employer as men; they are not as ambitious and career-oriented; they will leave the organization once they start a family; they are not geographically mobile; they cannot be decisive or assertive, and therefore would not be good managers; et cetera. And unfortunately, like any negative stereotype, damage is done on both the collective and the individual levels. Attitudes and cultures which pervade organizations become very important pieces of information for women looking to advance.

STRUCTURAL HURDLES IN THE CIVIL SERVICE

In the federal civil service there are different points at which barriers can exist. Barriers to entrance into the civil service, which exist for both women and men, start with a complex and esoteric staffing system. Not only is the process by which people acquire a civil service job complicated, but it is also based on competing goals. The staffing system has its foundation in several Merit Factors (see "Merit Principles" in *Bibliographies and Other General Resources* section), yet at the same time, the system supports such programs as Veterans Preference which tends to favor hiring men (see #98).

Occupational segregation is also a phenomenon that is well documented in the literature and borne out by personnel statistics. Women are more likely to be found in Administrative and Clerical occupations, and men dominate the Professional occupational groups. This translates into an average grade level for women in white-collar jobs of 7.3; for men the average grade is 10.3. Further, positions in male-dominated occupations in the civil service earn an average of 16.6% more than positions in female-dominated occupations (see #277).

Job evaluation systems have also come under attack for being gender biased (see, for example, #263). According to much of the research, job evaluation systems have historically placed a lower economic value on female-dominated occupations. The Factor Evaluation System (FES) is the system in the federal government through which most jobs are classified; evaluations are then translated into grade level and ultimately salary. Some assert that FES has perpetuated pay disparity (see #293). Others argue, conversely, that women are not valued less in the workplace, but rather they are steered into *occupations* which are valued less (see, for example, #269).

Introduction   xxiii

Finally, pay represents the culmination of all the structural and organizational factors that determine women's status in employment--the level at which they are recruited, the rate at which they are promoted, and the rewards which they are given. Pay inequity is the most tangible and overt disparity between men and women in the federal service. Some argue that there are patterns that point to discrimination against women which are causing economic disparity (see #264); others argue that education and experience account for most of the differences between the wages of men and women, and proactive policies to fix pay will not be effective (see #273). The "comparable worth" debate rages on in the literature and in the courts.

COMBATING DISCRIMINATION BASED ON SEX

All of these barriers to advancement, whether overt or subtle, can be described as discrimination based on sex. Sex discrimination in federal employment is actively combated with policies, processes and programs under the auspices of Affirmative Action and Equal Employment Opportunity. (This policy was first articulated by Executive Order 11375--see *Affirmative Action & Equal Employment Opportunity* chapter for text.)

And there are mixed reviews of the relative success of such programs to spur the advancement of women in the workplace. Some report a "backlash" from setting positions aside for particular groups, undermining the credibility of people who fill those positions even when they are qualified (see #137). Others argue that merit systems must have embedded in them the goal of creating a representative workforce, and Affirmative Action programs are an integral part of that pursuit (see #146).

Whether policies are proactive like Affirmative Action, reactive like Equal Employment Opportunity complaint processes, or more passive like natural incremental improvement in the status of women in the workforce, women continue to experience discrimination on the job. One such form of sex discrimination that has recently received a lot of attention is sexual harassment. The Clarence Thomas confirmation hearings before the United States Senate brought sexual harassment to the American living room and resulted in renewed attention to the dynamics involved (see #237).

The Merit Systems Protection Board reported in its 1988 study of sexual harassment in the federal workplace that 42% of the women responding to their survey had experienced some form of uninvited sexual attention, and only 21% of the respondents thought that sexual harassment was less of a problem now than it was five years ago (see #256). But as awareness of the problem grows, and as the courts define and redefine sexual harassment, formal policies and processes will be honed to protect women from this kind of discrimination in the workplace.

WOMEN REACHING FOR THE TOP

Despite the problems that exist, there are women who do reach the higher-echelon, higher-paying positions of the bureaucracy. These women have probably had to face many of the barriers articulated above, yet they have found viable strategies for advancing their careers. And once they "arrive," new issues and problems emerge.

Any federal manager must face the complexities of public policy problems, the uncertainties that arise with changing Administrations (which result in different employers), the Politics of tough decisions, and the pressure of shrinking budgets, fewer staff, and public accountability. Managing programs and people in the public sector presents many challenges to both women and men (see #35).

Since female managers are still relatively rare, women have had to model themselves after those who went before them--mostly men. And although this dynamic is changing, some women have felt forced to adopt some

Introduction xxv

traditionally "male" traits in order to survive in management. But as more and more women reach the higher levels of government, it will be easier to exert their personal styles in their positions. Traditionally "feminine traits" will not be eschewed as they have been.

In fact, traits frequently labeled "feminine" like building consensus, taking personal interest in employees, behaving cooperatively rather than competitively, and creating more open work environments are practices which are beginning to be admired in the workplace (see #56). With the projected changes to the cultural make-up of the federal workforce (see entry #72 and #77), it will be increasingly important to use nontraditional means of managing. This represents a new challenge for human resource and other managers, but perhaps it also represents an opportunity for women to showcase their natural managerial potential.

Some of the traits that men have traditionally brought to management will not lose their importance in the workplace of the future either. Much of the literature recognizes that both conventions have their place--both have something to offer the field of management and the operation of organizations. Women and men who are able to use the best of feminine traits and the best of masculine traits will be the most effective and successful managers (see, for example, #60).

As women reach the top levels of government, the possibility for more women reaching the top moves closer to reality. More women will have role-models and same-sex mentors from whom they can learn. Professional networks for women will also be more prevalent, and women will use their contacts from within their own ranks to help further the careers of others. In fact, women in executive positions in the government often cite their bosses and role-models (both male and female) as one of the most important factors in their advancement and success (see #24).

PREDICTIONS FOR THE FUTURE

Demographic changes predicted by several studies may also impact the status of women in the workplace. *Workforce 2000* (#72), for example, estimates that by the year 2000, about 47 percent of the workforce will be women, and 61 percent of women will be at work. And although some of the methodologies of this study have come into question, current data continue to show that women are comprising a growing proportion of graduates from professional schools. Women are also increasing their numbers in male-dominated occupations like law, accounting, computer science and business.

These predicted changes will not only foster continued social change vis-a-vis work and family issues, but economic trends will also reflect increased participation by women in the labor force. Policies and programs dealing with taxation, pensions, leave, hiring, compensation, and organizational structures may have to be re-thought to accommodate them.

Indeed, women in the federal civil service will continue to face many of the complex issues addressed by the literature that follows. The climb up the career ladder will continue to be replete with dilemmas and obstacles. Women will need to continue to develop viable strategies and coping mechanisms, and those who follow will need to learn from those who went before. Implications for women who aspire to enter the ranks of management or embark on a non-traditional career may be quite different in the future, however. As a "critical mass" of women develops at every level and in all occupations in the federal government, the road to the top may seem a little less rough.

Introduction xxvii

COMPOSITION OF THIS RESOURCE GUIDE & BIBLIOGRAPHY

The citations contained in this book are eclectic. Some come from private industry research and practice. My purpose in including these sources was to allow the reader to have comparable and contrastable information, but also to introduce issues which may arise, or are currently arising in the federal sector and have not yet appeared in the literature. I have excluded sources that dealt with issues that did not seem transferrable (e.g., advancement of women in sales positions).

I have also included sources from State and local government and International research where I felt comparison was possible. Government reports and relevant Congressional Hearings are also listed, as well as various documents (some verbatim) that are either interesting background or provide information about laws or Administrative processes. Organizational resources, relevant associations, and periodicals are also included with the subject area to which they are germane.

The topics covered come from experience and intuition about the issues that are important to women as they advance in the federal bureaucracy. I also solicited information from women's organizations about topics of import; and the topic list evolved, of course, as I did the preliminary searches.

The *Advancing Careers* chapter includes many "how-to" books and articles which suggest plans and strategies women can use to further their careers. Information on management styles and projected workforce changes are also included in this section. *Barriers To Advancement* covers much of the recent literature on the "Glass Ceiling" phenomenon including many of the factors believed to contribute to it.

The *Affirmative Action & Equal Employment Opportunity* chapter addresses issues related to laws and policies on discrimination as well as representation more generally. Similarly, *Sexual Harassment* covers literature on legal questions and the evolution of the definition of sexual harassment. The *Pay Equity* section skims the surface of the "comparable worth" literature--volumes have been written on this topic, this is just a taste.

The *Mentors & Networking* chapter deals with the importance as well as the pros and cons of having connections, and *Women in Non-Traditional Occupations* covers issues women in blue-collar, technical, and military occupations face. The *Work & Family* chapter deals with topics that any modern working parent confronts, it should be interesting to both women and men. Finally, *Bibliographies & Other General Resources* cites many of the compilations that relate to topics covered in the preceding chapters.

Most of the sources included are fairly current. Some of the topics covered have not emerged until recently; others deserve the most cutting-edge coverage. Where historical perspective was deemed appropriate, where a source is a classic in its field, or where the information contained in a source was thought especially relevant, I made exceptions. Sources basically cover the last five years of research. Since many of the topics are interrelated, some sources fit into more than one of the subjects covered. I have cross-listed them as appropriate.

ENVOI

This book is intended for researchers and practitioners alike. Some of the sources were found in academic journals; those interested in doing further research into the issues covered should find these citations a good starting place. Some of the entries come from popular literature. It is my hope that practitioners (employees and managers) will find this information useful in their daily conduct of business. Most of the sources are intended to "shed light" on the various issues women trying to advance in their careers in the federal civil service face. The information contained herein should serve to foster ideas about how to break down barriers to advancement and take positive steps to meet career goals.

career advancement for
women in the federal service

CHAPTER 1

Advancing Careers

"Now, we are becoming the men we wanted to marry." Gloria Steinem.

PLANNING & STRATEGIES

1. American Society for Public Administration, National Capital Area Chapter. *Breaking Through the Glass Ceiling: A Career Guide for Women in Government.* Washington: National Capital Area Chapter, ASPA, 1992.

   Through a cooperative effort of over 100 volunteers, this practical guide to advancement for women in the public service covers such topics as making a job change, necessary knowledge and skills, training opportunities, mentors and networking, balancing competing priorities, and the supervisor's perspective: what women need to know. Using data from focus groups conducted with high-level women and men in government, advice is given on the above topics through direct quotes and summaries of the issues.

2. Arroba, Tanya, and Kim James. "Are Politics Palatable to Women Managers? How Women Can Make Wise Moves at Work." *Women in Management Review* (UK). 3 (No. 3, 1988): 123-130.

Argues that three factors account for women's reluctance to engage in politics: perceptions of incompetence, lack of confidence, and distaste for political activity. Asserts that participating in political activity can be done without compromising personal ethics, and can even build on the "feminine" qualities that some women already bring to the job. Concludes that factors constraining some women's ability to read a political situation are: male dominance and operation of organizations, exclusion from informal networks, fear of power, and sexual politics.

3. Bergmann, Barbara R. *The Economic Emergence of Women.* New York: Basic Books, 1986.

A practical guide for women who want to achieve equality with men in the workforce and at home. Includes policy recommendations for improving the economic and social status of women.

4. Blanksby, Margaret. "In Their Own Words: The Clues to How to Develop Women Managers." *Women in Management Review* (UK). 3 (No. 2, 1987): 71-77.

One recent UK survey found that the number of women in full-time top management jobs has dropped from 9.7% to 5.8% in the last 10 years, with women as only 15% of middle and junior management. Stresses role models for aspiring managers, but argues that some of these models are intimidating to women. Women need positive images of management. One management model described includes the functions of planning, organizing, commanding, coordinating, and controlling. Because this model was developed by men, it can be argued that it requires the skills and use of "male attributes." The second model discussed presents a more balanced view of management.

5. Blessing, Buck. "Career Planning: Five Fatal Assumptions." *Training and Development Journal.* 40 (No. 9, 1986): 49-51.

Assumptions center on five common career-planning questions: 1) People want to know "where am I going?" 2) Is personal growth gradual or episodic? 3) Who is responsible for career planning? 4) Is career planning about the present or the future? 5) Is career planning about choice or about commitment?

6. Bremer, Kamala, and Deborah A Howe. "Strategies Used to Advance Women's Careers in the Public Service: Examples from Oregon." *Public Administration Review.* 48 (November/December 1988): 957-961.

Case study of seven local, state, and federal agencies in Oregon that have track records of success in moving women into management positions. Top managers, personnel officers, and promoted women managers are interviewed to identify the strategies which were instrumental in the advancement of women.

7. Brennan, Eileen M., and Julie M. Rosenzweig. "Women and Work: Toward a New Developmental Model." *Families in Society.* 71 (November 1990): 524-533.

Proposes a model that ascribes women's growth and development of self-understanding to work as well as personal and social relationships. Gives practical implications using a case study of a 35-year-old working woman.

8. Cooper, Cary L., and Marilyn J. Davidson. *Women in Management: Career Development for Managerial Success.* Heinemann, William, 1984.

Examines several British and American female executives and the career planning strategies they employ. Concentrates on strategies that are successful in advancing careers.

9. DiPrete, Thomas A. "Horizontal and Vertical Mobility in Organizations." *Administrative Sciences Quarterly.* 32 (Summer 1987): 422-444.

Analyzes hiring in one federal agency between 1975 and 1978. Concludes that there is a relationship between the structural characteristics of organizations vis-a-vis career ladders and the rate at which employees advance. Implications for mobility are discussed.

10. DiPrete, Thomas A. "The Professionalization of Administration and Equal Employment Opportunity in the U.S. Federal Government." *American Journal of Sociology.* 93 (July 1987): 119-140.

Analyzes the 15 largest federal agencies covering the period 1962-77 on the rate at which lower-level employees moved into entry-level administrative positions. Results suggest that upward-mobility programs initiated during these years allowed a higher percentage of entry-level administrative positions to be filled internally. Argues that women and minorities benefitted most from these programs and suggests implications for future advancement.

11. Fields, Daisy B. *A Woman's Guide to Moving Up in Business & Government.* Englewood Cliffs, N.J.: Prentice-Hall, 1983.

General guide to organizational issues of which women must be aware in order to advance their careers. Gives practical advice about a variety of career-enhancing tactics including mentors, networks and developmental activities.

12. Figart, Deborah M. "Collective Bargaining and Career Development for Women in the Public Sector." *Journal of Collective Negotiations in the Public Sector.* 18 (No. 4, 1989): 301-313.

Argues that unions and employers in the public sector provide better career opportunities for women, and are, therefore, in a better position to achieve pay equity. New York State's Clerical and Secretarial Employee Advancement Program is set forth as a model to help women advance in the workplace. Discusses several methods of career advancement including cross-over method, bridge method, and skills-upgrading method. Some specific approaches addressed for helping women advance include restructuring jobs, developing education and training programs for women, and creating bridge occupations.

13. Forbes, J. Benjamin, and James E. Piercy. "Rising to the Top: Executive Women in 1983 and Beyond." *Business Horizons.* 26 (September/October 1983): 38-47.

Based on a study of over 1,000 female executives. Examines their characteristics, styles and backgrounds.

14. Fraser, Jill A. *The Best U.S. Cities for Working Women.* Bergenfield, N.J.: National American Library.

Offers comprehensive information of different geographic areas based on employment patterns and information from interviews with women around the country. Provides general information on the most marketable skills, networks, and places to live for women planning career strategies.

15. Galagan, Patricia. "A Most Important Development." *Training and Development Journal* 40 (May 1986): 4.

Notes that women are having difficulty moving beyond the first level of management, but there are other successes to be seen. Department of Labor statistics are cited that show women encumbering the majority of professional jobs, and starting their own businesses at five times the rate of men. Concludes that the "glass ceiling" will not stop women; women are and will continue to look for alternatives to male-centered equality.

16. Greenhaus, Jeffrey H. *Career Management*. The Dryden Press, Holt, Rinehart and Winston, 1987.

Provides a model of career management which specifies how people can collect information, gain insight into themselves and their environment, develop appropriate goals and strategies, and obtain useful feedback regarding their efforts. Demonstrates principles by examining hypothetical but realistic career portraits of managers, outlining their career history, their personal values, etc. Exercises for using the model of career management are included.

17. Grossman, Hildreth Y., and Nia Lane Chester. *The Experience and Meaning of Work in Women's Lives*. Erlbaum, 1990

Partial contents: Women Supporting Women: Secretaries and Their Bosses, by Virginia E. O'Leary and Jeanette Ickovics; Achievement Motivation and Employment Decisions: Portraits of Women with Young Children, by Nia Lane Chester; Crossing Boundaries Between Professional and Private Life, by Judith Richter; Blue-Collar Women: Paying the Price at Home on the Job, by Jean Reith Schroedel.

18. Gutek, Barbara A., and Laurie Larwood. *Women's Career Development*. Newbury Park, CA: Sage Publications, Inc., 1987.

Outlines new and innovative approaches that researchers are taking in the analysis of women's career development (e.g., experiments, cohort analyses, surveys, etc.). These new approaches, it is argued, will shed new light on the directions of women's careers. Suggestions are made for further innovation in research and more new directions for women's careers.

19. Harvey, Carol. "How to Succeed When It's Trying." *Bureaucrat*. 20 (Fall 1991): 33-36.

Interview with Harriett G. Jenkins, Assistant Administrator for Equal Opportunity Programs at the National Aeronautics and Space Administration, one of the few women to break into the Senior Executive Service (SES) during the 1970's. Issues of career advancement for women in the federal service as well as the equal employment opportunity program are discussed.

20. Henning, M., and Jardin, A. *The Managerial Woman*. New York: Simon and Schuster Pocket Book. 1977.

Analyzes characteristics of successful women by looking at similarities in their upbringing, education, and socialization. Also discusses alternatives that both men and women have to ensure successful careers for women.

21. Jacobson, Aileen. *Women in Charge: Dilemmas of Women in Authority*. New York: Van Nostrand Reinhold Company, 1985.

Looks at the backgrounds of 35 women in positions of authority to discover reasons behind problems women in powerful positions face. Discusses issues surrounding the general lack of training (from childhood) in the development of managerial skills and attitudes in women. Examines stereotypes of women in charge and outstanding women throughout history who have not been successful. The general goal is to provide

insight for all women into increasing their competence and confidence. Advice on developing assertive behavior, giving and receiving criticism, dealing with sexual harassment, overcoming stereotypes, and balancing work and family demands is given through anecdotes and lessons learned.

22. Kelly, Rita Mae. *The Gendered Economy: Work, Careers, and Success*. Newbury Park CA: Sage Publications, 1991.

Outlines the many factors that influence women's advancement in business and the professions. Discusses the relationship between gender and socialization, the sex-role spillover, and the "glass ceiling."

23. Lee, R.A., and Piper, J. "The Graduate Promotion Process: Understanding the Soft Side." *Personnel Review* 18 (No. 3, 1989): 36-47.

Highlights the importance of the subjective, informal and political aspects of the promotion process. Points out that a lot of employees perceive that the ability to get promoted is a separate ability from that required to do the job. Argues that the "soft side" of promotion (i.e., understanding culture, labeling, sponsors, etc.) is the key to managing the promotion process.

24. Little, Danity M. "Shattering the Glass Ceiling." *Bureaucrat*. 20 (Fall 1991): 24-28.

Using questionnaire data from 645 Senior Executive Service (SES) women, issues of how executives learn, how they develop their careers, and what makes a difference in the highest ranks within their organizations are explored. Results show that there are common "key events" and "lessons learned" by these women that shed light on how to shatter the glass ceiling in the federal government. One common theme discussed by these women relates to the influence of bosses and role models. Concludes that these factors need to be accounted for as women with high potential for management are developed by their organizations.

25. Lewis, Gregory. "Gender and Promotions: Promotion Chances of White Men and Women in Federal White-Collar Employment." *Journal of Human Resources.* 21 (1986): 406-419.

   Using data from the Central Personnel Data File for 1973 to 1982, promotion potential for men and women in the federal government is examined. Data are divided into professional/ administrative and technical/clerical positions. Concludes that gender has little effect on promotion opportunities within occupations; however, women seem to have more difficulty breaking into particular positions than being promoted within them once they are there.

26. Lewis, Gregory. "Men and Women in Federal Employment: Placements, Promotions and Occupations." Syracuse University, Ph.D. Dissertation, 1984.

   Provides a history of women's status in federal employment. Examines the impact of Veterans' preference and occupational choice and placement on initial grade and promotions. Concludes that, since veterans tend to be at lower grades than non-veterans, Veterans' preference is not a major factor in the lower standing of women. Attributes the lower entry grades of women to their lower educational attainment and lower pay they receive during the time between school and federal employment. Occupational segregation in federal employment is also strongly related to women's lower status at the time of the study. Argues that prospects for women in federal employment are virtually the same as men's, and perhaps a little better.

27. London, Manuel, and Stephen A. Stumpf. "Promotion Decisions." *Management Decision,* 24 (No. 1, 1986): 21-25.

Using interview and survey data, combined with results from a decision-making simulation completed by managers at three organizational levels, examines how management promotion decisions are made in a large organization. Discusses implications of the results in terms of how individuals needs and desires formulated during career planning may be taken into account during the promotion process.

28. Markham, William T., Scott J. South., Charles M. Bonjean, and Judy Corder. "Gender and Opportunity in the Federal Bureaucracy." *American Journal of Sociology,* 91 (No. 1, 1985): 129-150.

Tests Rosabeth Moss Kanter's (1977) hypotheses that (a) promotion opportunity in organizations is related to several adaptive attitudes and behaviors, (b) women have less promotion opportunity, (c) women are more likely to display the adaptations, and (d) these gender differences are eliminated when opportunity is controlled. Using survey data from 897 employees in 6 offices of a government agency on chances of promotion to specific positions, it is revealed that low opportunity was moderately related to dissatisfaction with the promotion system. Concludes that, although gender is closely related to occupational level, and the segregation of women in lower-level career ladders, promotion opportunities for both sexes within their specific career ladders is relatively equal. Results also show a modest relationship to desire for security and interpersonal support on the job.

29. Markham, William T. "Sex, Relocation and Occupational Advancement: The 'Real Cruncher' for Women." *Women and Work: An Annual Review.* 2 (1987): 207-231.

Reviews the literature on the relationships between sex, geographic mobility and job advancement, and analyzes the effects of physical relocation on the careers of women and men. Evidence suggests that relocation enhances the careers of those who move in order to advance their careers. The evidence further suggests that women move less often to advance their careers, and they are less willing to move than men. There is no clear cut answer about why these differences exist; a call for further study is made.

30. McBroom, Patricia A. *The Third Sex: The New Professional Woman.* New York: William Morrow, 1986.

   Discusses gender identity, role changes, marriage, and child rearing with a focus on the self-determination and power of women in the workforce.

31. Marshall, J. "A Testing Time Full of Potential." *Women in Management Review* 1 (Spring 1985): 5-14.

   Discusses four trends in the context of how they will help women advance into management--the movement away from male models of management to diverse models, the creation of "women-only spares," the increasing identification and support among women, and developing opportunities for dialogue between women and men.

32. Morphet, Janice. "Women in Local Government: A Case Study." *Public Money and Management.* 10 (Spring 1990): 57-59.

   Charts the career paths of four women chief executives in Great Britain.

33. Nachmias, David. "The Quality of Work Life in the Federal Bureaucracy: Conceptualization and Measurement." *American Review of Public Administration.* 18 (June 1988): 165-173.

   Using data from over 13,000 federal employees, the issue of Quality of Work Life (QWL) is explored. Results show five distinct dimensions of QWL. The most significant factor measures different aspects of supervision--especially the extent to which supervisors outline clear goals and performance criteria. The second most important factor relates to relationships with co-workers, the third includes items measuring attributes of the work itself--whether it is meaningful, satisfying and challenging. The fourth factor is a measurement of work group relationships, and the fifth is an economic dimension of work. Concludes that Policymakers should use this information when making decisions about work life issues for federal employees.

34. Parks, Gregory. "Gender and Promotions: Promotion Chances of White Men and Women in Federal White-Collar Employment." *Journal of Human Resources.* 21 (No. 3, 1986): 406-419.

Using Central Personnel Data File data from 1974 to 1982, examines the relationship between gender and promotion possibilities for General Schedule employees. Concludes that minor differences exist in promotion rates of men and women.

35. Posner, Barry Z., and Warren H. Schmidt. "Government Morale and Management: A Survey of Federal Executives." *Public Personnel Management.* 17 (Spring 1988): 21-27.

Using survey data from over 800 executives in the federal government, explores variables contributing to general morale. Executives are questioned about experiences under administrations from Lyndon B. Johnson to Ronald Reagan. Issues like working conditions, organizational climate, job recognition, clarity of purpose, feedback, and influence are examined. Results show that things have deteriorated steadily since the Johnson Administration. Discovers that problems affecting morale in public organizations seem to be: unclear organizational goals, lack of human resource orientation, and lack of support from superiors and the public. Concludes that the role of future administrations should be to return pride, purpose and clear goals to the government.

36. Poston, Ersa H. "Working for Aunt Sam." *Civil Service Journal.* 18 (January/March 1978): 14-17.

Discusses the role of women within the civil service system. Asserts that there is a need for change within the system and suggests that such changes should include a greater commitment to affirmative action recruiting and the training of women for management positions. Also asserts that women have an organizational responsibility to help change the system and a personal responsibility to accept leadership and plot their career directions wisely.

37. Riccucci, Norma M. *Women, Minorities, and Unions in the Public Sector* (Contributions in Labor Studies No. 28). Westport, CT: Greenwood Press, 1990.

Outlines the legal, political, and historical aspects of union involvement in female and minority employment in the public sector, and argues that the role of unions, though sometimes unnoticed has been rather significant. Partial contents: Women, Minorities, and Joint Labor-Management Cooperation; Women in Uniformed Service Jobs: the Role of Unions; Unions and Comparable Worth.

38. Rogalin, Wilma C., and Arthur R. Pell. *Women's Guide to Management Positions.* New York: Simon and Schuster, Inc., 1975.

Outlines strategies to help women realize their potential of achieving higher status and higher-paying positions in business, government and in the professions. Includes guidelines to women who seek advancement, as well as an overall self-evaluation guide.

39. Rumberger, Russell W. *Social Mobility and Public Sector Employment* (Project report no. 83-A2). Stanford, California

Institute for Research on Educational Finance and Governance, 1983.

States that the government has provided one-quarter of all new jobs and one-third of all high-level, professional jobs in the economy between 1960 and 1980. Discusses the role government, as an employer, has played in providing opportunities for women and minorities. Argues that, although the wage gap exists in all sectors of employment, the public sector discriminates less, in general, and therefore may provide "better" employment for women and minorities.

40. Scott, Karen R. "Introduction to the Women In Government Forum." *Bureaucrat*. 20 (Fall 1991): 3-4.

Outlines the progress women have made in the federal civil service, but concludes that further strides must be made. Discusses the results of a survey conducted by the organization Federally Employed Women (FEW) and the Federal Women's Program (FWP) which showed that women remain in the lower-echelon positions in the federal government, and that discrimination is still a pervasive problem. Concludes by outlining the purpose of the Women in Government Forum and issues that will be discussed.

41. Sheldon, Suzanne E., and Roger A. Sheldon. *Women in Government*. Lincolnwood, IL: VGM Career Horizons, 1984.

Includes a section on employment and appointment terminology in the federal government, as well as specific training curricula for women interested in public service. Covers issues for women in all levels of government: local, county, federal (legislative and executive). Gives general advice about getting a job in the public service; provides vignettes of successful women public officials.

42. Spenner, Kenneth I., and Rachel A. Rosenfeld. "Women, Work, and Identities." *Social Science Research* 19 (September 1990): 266-299.

Examines the life histories of 2,536 women at age 17 (1966) and again at age 30 (1979). Tests the concept of identity to determine the frequency with which women change career positions. The research shows that transitions into and out of identity states are functions of fixed and changing personal resources, changes in stage of the family life cycle, rewards and opportunities associated with the present job and career line, and several forms of "duration dependence."

43. Stamp, Gillian. "Some Observations on Career Paths of Women." *The Journal of Applied Behavioral Science*, 22 (No. 4, 1986): 385-396.

Using a sample of 168 women managers and military officers from the United Kingdom and United States, hypothesizes that connections between individuals and organizations influence career paths. A model of structural and individual development is developed which integrates the abilities an individual brings to the job with the organizations' standards. Results show that organizational barriers have different natures and impacts on the realization of women's competence and abilities at different levels of organizations.

44. Stead, B.A. *Women in Management*. New Jersey: Prentice Hall, 1985.

Provides research findings on women in management as well as practical advice and strategies for women on how to succeed. Includes several "articles" on sex-role stereotyping, networking socialization, political awareness, tokenism, sex bias in evaluation, subtle forms of sex discrimination related to promotional patterns and supervisory feedback, "critical mass" theory (i.e., as more women enter organizations job discrimination will decline markedly).

45. Sutton, Charlotte Decker, and Kris K. Moore. "Attitudes Toward Executive Women: Do They Differ Geographically?" *Personnel Administrator* 31 (May 1986): 75-88.

Surveys 782 male and female executives in different geographic locations. Outcomes suggest that women executives in the western and eastern areas of the United States have more opportunities.

46. U.S. Office of Personnel Management. Federal Women's Program. *Putting Women in Their Place.* Washington: G.P.O. 1979.

Describes the charter and activities of the Federal Women's Program as well as the legal authority and requirements of the Program which was established to help women advance in careers in the federal service. Contains general information on American women, the history of women in the federal service, and the responsibilities of Federal Women's Program Managers.

47. U.S. Office of Personnel Management. *Federal Career Directory, A Guide to College Students.* Washington: G.P.O., 1990. (Superintendent of Documents; stock # 006-000-00900-0)

Lists federal agencies and the dominant occupations therein. Gives basic information about applying for federal jobs, as well as organizational structures.

48. Ward, T. *Smart Women at Work: 12 Steps to Career Breakthrough.* Chicago: Contemporary Books, 1987.

Deals with confidence and self-esteem issues. A practical guide to helping women make decisions about issues of job vs. career.

49. ---. *Women in Government; Your Guide to More than 600 Top Women in the Federal Government* (From the Office of Sarah Weddington, The White House). Washington, 1980.

Prepared by the Interdepartmental Task Force on Women, lists women who were at the GS-16 level and above at the time.

50. ---. "Women in Management." *Journal of Business Ethics*. 9 (April/May 1990): 243-453.

Twenty-one papers presented at a conference sponsored jointly by Mount Saint Vincent University and the Canadian Federation of Deans of Management and Administrative Studies, April 27-29, 1988. Survey of existing research; questions in the areas of careers, leadership, education and training, and entrepreneurship. Partial contents: "Androgyny and Leadership Style," by Karen Korabik; "Mentoring in Organizations: Implications for Women," by R. J. Burke and C. A. McKeen.

MANAGEMENT STYLE

51. ---. "A Matter of Personal Ability, Not Gender." *Management Solutions*. 32 (November 1987): 38-45.

Delineates theories of "masculine" and "feminine" management styles, and argues that recent thinking supports the idea that "good" managers possess a combination of these traits. Cites a 1980 study which concludes that men and women do not differ in management technique or style. Argues that the workplace should stereotype-free; this can be accomplished by developing mentoring programs, opening lines of communication, and monitoring the development of female managers.

52. Cleveland, Ceil. "Campus CEO." *Working Woman*. 16 (December 1991): 60-63.

Profiles Donna Shalala, the first woman to lead a Big 10 University as the chancellor of the University of Wisconsin at Madison. Shalala uses a management style that has served her well in the federal government, city politics, and academia, and claims that good management means "giving power away." In addition, she typically attacks issues by building consensus with the appropriate stakeholders. Shalala also believes that mentors are not just valuable, they are necessary.

53. Coppolino, Yolanda, and Carol B. Seath. "Women Managers: Fitting the Mould or Moulding the Fit?" *Equal Opportunities International* (UK). 6 (No. 3, 1987): 4-10.

Reports results of a questionnaire administered to 131 female managers on decision making, interpersonal conflicts, leadership traits, change, and barriers to success. The respondents were on average between 30-40 years old, and 71% had a university education. Most worked in organizations with 5,000-25,000 employees and defined their organizations as traditionally structured hierarchically with rigid reporting structures and relationships. When asked about considerations they might bring to their decision-making processes, 121 ranked relational considerations as either their first or second choice. The introspective part of the questionnaire showed that, generally, women are very aware of the behavior changes required to function successfully in organizations. Some evidence suggests that respondents are changing the culture and structure of their organizations by bringing feminine viewpoints to their managerial roles.

54. Duerst Lahti, Georgia, and Cathy Marie. "Gender and Style in Bureaucracy." *Women & Politics*. 10 (No. 4, 1990): 67-120.

Using data from a survey of Wisconsin professional and executive civil servants, argues that the best civil servants are gender neutral; placing equal emphasis on feminine and masculine traits. Finds that women and men cross gender stereotypes in their styles as well as in their perceptions of good leaders and co-workers. Women tend to avoid negative masculine and feminine traits and embrace traits valued most by bureaucrats, especially those important for achieving the desired organizational results.

55. Gregory, A. "Where Are We Coming From and Where Are We Going? Theoretical, Research and Methodological Perspectives on Women in Management." *Women in Management Research Symposium*, Mount Saint Vincent University, Nova Scotia, 1988: pp. 1.1-1.15.

Reviews the literature on gender differences and gender stereotyping. Suggestions are given for future research directions that would contribute to a better understanding of women in management, and the issues that they face.

56. Handley, Elisabeth A. "Women as Managers and Managing Women." *Bureaucrat*. 20 (Fall 1991): 15-18.

Using interview data from 11 women and 9 men, women's management styles are examined. Two of the respondents feel that there is no difference in the management style of men and women. However most describe female supervisors as differing from men in a positive way. Women are reported to take more of an interest employees as people, are better able to communicate, and create more open, friendly work environments. Seventy-five percent of the respondents reported that working for women is not harder or easier than working for men, and 85% have no preference about whether their immediate supervisor is a man or a woman. Recommends that training for both male and female managers could help develop more of the positive qualities attributed to female supervisors.

57. Hearn, Jeff. "Leading Questions for Men: Men's Leadership, Feminist Challenges, and Men's Responses." *Equal Opportunity International* (UK). 8 (No. 1, 1989): 3-11.

Introductory article of a special issue on "men, masculinities and leadership" which provides some background information for following articles. Outlines major social changes that have contributed to the disassociation of leadership and maleness. Discusses the nature of feminism, and feminist challenges to men and leadership.

58. Kazemek, Edward A. "Interactive Leadership Gaining Sway in the 1990s." *Healthcare Financial Management*. 45 (June 1991): 16.

Reviews Judy B. Rosener's (1990) characterization of female leadership as "interactive" and male leadership as "command-and-control." Rosener suggests that interactive (i.e., female) leadership is more effective as the workplace changes so rapidly in the 1990s. Interactive leaders are different from command-and-control leaders in that they: 1) encourage participation, 2) share power and information willingly, and 3) enhance the self-worth of others. Concludes by discussing implications for health care leaders.

59. Kelly, Rita Mae, Mary M. Hale, and Jane Burgess. "Gender and Managerial/Leadership Styles: A Comparison of Arizona Public Administrators." *Women & Politics*. 11 (No. 2, 1991): 19-39.

Study of variations in male and female behavioral styles of management and leadership in high-level state government administrators in Arizona. Assesses differences in how men and women deal with power, subordinates, and relate with one another. Emphasizes the difficulty women have adopting typical male behavior.

60. Korabik, Karen, and Roya Ayman. "Should Women Managers Have to Act Like Men?" *Journal of Management Development* (UK). 8 (No. 6, 1989): 23-32.

Analyzes comments about management style of 30 women managers in Canada. Results show that women with "masculine styles" frequently describe themselves as "overly directive" and "lacking emotional sensitivity;" those with "feminine styles" describe themselves as "overly passive and accommodating" and "lacking in task orientation." Women managers who are characterized as "androgynous" describe themselves as able to strike an appropriate balance between assertiveness and cooperation. The supervisors of androgynous women managers also rate them as more effective than their masculine- and feminine-style counterparts. Similarly, androgynous women are perceived as superior in decision making, problem-solving ability, and the ability to listen effectively than masculine women managers, and as more influential and fair than feminine women managers. Concludes that both masculine and feminine characteristics are necessary for excellence.

61. Maupin, Rebekah J. "The Best of Both Sexes: Managers Who Embrace Both Male and Female Traits Are Happier on the Job." *Management World.* 16 (November-December 1987): 18.

Reports that a combination of masculine and feminine traits is the best formula for being a successful and satisfied manager. Advocates androgyny (i.e., recognizing facts and feelings; using both logic and intuition).

62. Morrison, Ann M., Randall P. White, and Ellen Van Velsor. "Executive Women: Substance Plus Style." *Psychology Today.* 21 (August 1987): 18-26.

Analyzes characteristics considered necessary by people responsible for identifying and selecting women for executive jobs. Characteristics named include: the ability to take risks and be consistently outstanding; the ability to be tough without sacrificing femininity; being ambitious without expecting equal treatment to men; and accepting responsibility but following the advice of others. Concludes that these competing expectations, which are almost paradoxical in nature, have led to a work environment for women executives that is different from that of men.

63. Nelton, Sharon. "Men, Women & Leadership." *Nation's Business*. 79 (May 1991): 16-22.

Argues that all leadership is becoming more "feminized" because it makes good business sense. Predicts that men will become freer to use "feminine" tools of interactive and consensus-building leadership, and women will use styles that are more reflective of their own personalities.

64. Pitcher, Fiona. "Using Women's Wiles." *Business* (UK). May, 1988, pp 90-93.

Profiles the Stuart Crystal Company in Stourbridge (UK) which employs a management approach based on compromise and cooperation instead of confrontation. This involves the manager who can call on the best of both male and female management skills, according to the situation encountered. Cites research conducted at the Cranfield Institute of Technology which showed that most men are good with "systems and procedures," but they are also prone to make decisions too quickly, and are less skilled at handling relationships at work. Faults attributed to women included advertising their own mistakes and not being "single-minded." Stuart Crystal has started using female supervisors. The company believes that women will bring the ability to search for consensus rather than "score points" to the workplace.

65. Rosener, Judy B. "Ways Women Lead." *Harvard Business Review*. 68 (November/December 1990): 119-125.

Argues that there is a "second wave" of women who are making it into top management by drawing on the skills and attitudes they developed from their experience as women, and by eschewing management and leadership styles that men have traditionally used. Cites a recent survey of men and women leaders in which men described themselves as "transactional" leaders; and women described themselves as "transformational" leaders (i.e., convincing subordinates to transform their own self-interest into the interest of the group through concern for a broader goal). Concludes that women make efforts to encourage participation and share both power and information.

66. Sargeant, Alice. *The Androgynous Manager*. New York: Amacom, 1981.

Argues that the management qualities organizations will value will not be traditionally "male" traits which tend to be command-and-control styles. Leaders and managers will be more effective if they focus on interdependence and support rather than competition.

67. Sharma, Sarla. "Psychology of Women in Management: A Distinct Feminine Leadership." *Equal Opportunities International* (UK). 9 (No. 2, 1990): 13-18.

Argues that women managers who possess certain distinctly feminine traits may be better prepared to cope with the challenges of the future than many traditional males. Skills that women were previously encouraged to leave behind as they entered management are now being recognized as critical to the health and viability of their organizations. Cites several reasons for the effectiveness of feminine leadership. Some of these include: a strong desire to succeed in a male-dominated environment, endurance for stress, ability to manage diverse tasks, and intuition and problem-solving skills. Concludes that the full potential of feminine leadership will only be realized when a large number of women managers begin to assert their true identity and use their unique talents.

WORKFORCE CHANGES

68. Brunet, Jean, and Serge Proulx. "Formal Versus Grass-Roots Training: Women, Work, and Computers." *Journal of Communication.* 39 (Summer 1989): 77-84.

    Examines several programs that offer microcomputing training. Results show that men use different kinds of computer training programs to advance their careers but women use them to catch up and survive economically in a changed workplace.

69. Drygulski, Barbara Wright, ed. *Women, Work, and Technology: Transformations.* Ann Arbor, MI: The University of Michigan Press, 1989.

    Discusses the many forces that affect the lives of women including social, economic, and technological change. An analysis of these influences is undertaken.

70. Freeman, Sue J.M. *Managing Lives: Corporate Women and Social Change.* Amherst, MA: The University of Massachusetts Press, 1989.

    Outlines the social and demographic changes that women in the workforce must face, specifically women in management. Discusses how societal change has affected the lives of women within and outside organizations, and provides analyses of what this change will continue to mean in the future.

71. Guinn, Stephen L. "The Changing Workforce." *Training & Development Journal.* 43 (December 1989): 36-39.

Because of the predicted changes in new entrants into the workforce by the year 2000, argues that recruiting in the labor market will require attention to the changed needs of employees. Examples cited relate mostly to different, more flexible benefits. Also gives the example of a new policy being adopted by many private-sector companies of a two-track career plan that includes the so called "Mommy Track," for people who want to work part-time to allow more time for their families.

72. Johnston, William B. *Workforce 2000*. Washington: Hudson Institute, 1987.

Predicts various demographic and cultural shifts in the U.S. workforce in the coming decades. Among the significant changes are the record numbers of female and minority (and international) workers entering the labor force, and the aging of the workforce as the baby-boom generation moves into retirement. Recommendations for dealing with these changes are given.

73. Kamerman, Sheila, and Alfred J. Kahn. *The Responsive Workplace: Employers and a Changing Labor Force*. New York: Columbia University Press, 1987.

Citing a national study of workforce trends, and using supportive data, argues that employers must respond to workforce changes through responsive employment policies and practices. Employers must be especially sensitive to the needs of women who are being radically affected by societal changes.

74. Kraft, Joan F., and Jurg K. Siegenthaler. "Office Automation, Gender, and Change: An Analysis of the Management Literature." *Science, Technology, and Human Values: Journal of the Society for Social Studies of Science*. 14 (Spring 1989): 195-212.

Examines the consequences of computerization for women who do information work. Compares research findings in general social science and business and management periodical literature.

75. Levine, Charles H. "Career Success in the Future." *Bureaucrat.* 16 (Spring 1987): 37-39.

Argues that anyone doing career planning must know where the risks and rewards will be. Focuses on changes in the past decade to federal government career patterns including: greater use and acceptance of an "administrative presidency," more freedom of movement within the federal system mostly because of the revised federal retirement system (Federal Employee Retirement System--FERS), and the increasing privatization of federal services. Argues that it will be important for federal employees to do extra-organizational networking, and pay attention to political contacts at the higher levels. Also argues that, although it will be difficult, it is important for career planners to maintain and strengthen internal processes and procedures while being flexible, adaptable, and innovative.

76. Richter, Werner. *The Changing Role of Women in Society: A Documentation of Current Research; Research Projects in Progress 1984-1987.* East Berlin, Germany (Democratic Republic): Akademie Verlag, Leipziger Strasse 3-4. 1989.

Inventories social science research in Europe on women's role in society. Includes national reports on 17 European countries and the former Soviet Union. Coordinated by the European Coordination Centre for Research and Documentation in Social Sciences (Vienna Centre).

77. U.S. Office of Personnel Management. *Civil Service 2000.* Washington: G.P.O., 1988.

Report commissioned by the U.S. Office of Personnel Management as a follow-on the *Workforce 2000* (See entry 72). Similar projections for demographic and cultural changes were made for the federal civil service, along with predictions about potential shifts of employees away from Defense to domestic agencies.

78. Wooldridge, Blue, and Jennifer Wester. "The Turbulent Environment of Public Personnel Administration: Responding to the Challenge of the Changing Workplace of the Twenty-First Century." *Public Personnel Management.* 20 (Summer 1991): 207-224.

In the context of the expected demographic changes predicted in the next decades, argues that employers must implement innovative and responsive personnel practices in order to keep up with this rapid change. Argues that local governments and local public personnel administrators will need to develop strategies for dealing with change and diversity. Some such strategies include: encouraging employee input into agency decisions, using educational leave or tuition reimbursement, employee training, and sick leave for maternity purposes to meet the needs of workers (and keep them satisfied with their jobs), and to benefit the operation and productivity of local governments.

79. Wright, Barbara Drygulski. *Women, Work, and Technology: Transformations.* University of Michigan Press (Women and Culture Series), 1987.

Based on papers presented at a conference on Women, Work and Technology, held at the University of Connecticut in October, 1984. Gives historical perspectives; experience of women office workers, including those working with computers.

80. Hyworon, Zorianna L. "Women, Computers and Change: The Impact of Computers on Women in Large Organizations." *Optimum: A Forum for Management.* 15 (No. 1, 1984): 49-61.

Concentrates primarily on women office workers, and how computers have changed their jobs and their quality of work life.

CHAPTER 2

Barriers To Advancement

"Ten thousand women marched through the streets of London [in support of women's suffrage] saying: 'We will not be dictated to,' and then went off to become stenographers." G.K. Chesterton.

THE "GLASS CEILING" AND OTHER IMPEDIMENTS

81. Abbott, Linda M.C. "Women, Work, and Self-Esteem: A Bibliographic Essay." *Choice.* October, 1987. pp 265-274.

    Discusses societal responses that prompt negative attitudes toward women in the workplace. Analyzes the literature relating to women at work and how they view themselves.

82. Andrew, C., C. Coderre, and A. Denis. "Stop or Go: Reflections of Women Managers on Factors Influencing Their Career Development." *Journal of Business Ethics.* 9 (No. 4, 1990): 361-367.

Using a sample of 214 intermediate and senior women managers in the public and private sectors in Ontario and Quebec, Canada, analyzes barriers and facilitators to advancement. Results indicate that managers see a variety of "structural" elements more often as obstacles to career advancement than as facilitators to advancement. The factor seen most often as an obstacle was the small number of women managers in an organization. Although obstacles were not perceived to be caused by women, respondents tended to focus on the attitudes of their colleagues-- something that they perceived to be changeable.

83. Berman, Melissa A. "Talking Through Glass Walls." *Across the Board*. 25 (No. 8, 1988): 26-29.

Analyzes a phenomenon many women face on the job of not being heard or paid attention to when they try to participate in work-related discussions. Argues that half of the topics women raise fail to generate conversation, but nearly all the subjects introduced by men lead to discussion, including some that women had unsuccessfully broached. Reasons and implications related to this phenomenon are discussed.

84. Bhatnagar, D. "Professional Women in Organizations: New Paradigms for Research and Action." *Sex Roles*. 18 (March 1988): 343-355.

Reviews research on some of the major issues encountered by professional women in the workplace (e.g., social isolation, non-availability of mentors, tokenism, sex-role stereotyping and discrimination through under-rating and underpaying). Argues that explanations for these problems usually center on "person-centered" interpretations or "situation-specific" interpretations. Suggests that examining these issues as "sub-system" issues of an organization rather than as issues of concern to a subgroup could lead to more comprehensive organizational solutions. Argues that the impact of such problems should be examined vis-a-vis the organization as a whole.

85. Cannings, Kathy. "Managerial Promotion: The Effects of Socialization, Specialization, and Gender." *Industrial and Labor Relations Review.* 42 (October 1988): 77-89.

Using responses from a questionnaire sent to managers in a large Canadian corporation, finds that women were only 80% as likely to be promoted in any given year than their male counterparts. Discusses the importance of factors like socialization, education, and productivity on promotion, and concludes that gender still has a sizable impact on a manager's chance to be promoted.

86. Col, Jeanne Marie. *Barriers to Women's Advancement in Administration and Management.* Unpublished Manuscript. Springfield, IL: Sangamon State University, 1985.

Outlines and discusses the wide variety of factors that inhibit the progress of women in the workforce. Study of women which finds that performance and job evaluation systems, designed to accurately reflect promotion potential, often use criteria like personality and appearance. Also discusses perceptual difference of men and women related to the advancement of women. Men tend to believe that there are not enough women in the promotional "pipeline," that women lack training and educational qualifications, and that individual personality traits serve as barriers to women; women believe that personality traits, discrimination and negative stereotypes inhibit their progress. Concludes that women are often excluded from developmental opportunities as well (e.g., travel to conferences) which inhibits their ability to assimilate into professional networks, thus stunting their career growth.

87. Cote-O'Hara, Jocelyn, Jean Edmonds and Edna McKenzie. *The Report of the Task Force on Barriers to Women in the Public Service: Beneath the Veneer.* Ottawa: Canadian Government Publishing Centre. 1990.

Reports the findings of a task force formed by the Canadian government to study issues women face in their federal civil service. The group's charter included: 1) identification and ranking of barriers to advancement for women; 2) identification of occupational groups where women have particularly low pay and low status; 3) examination of the experiences of those women in nontraditional occupations or in predominantly male organizational units. Research was executed using surveys, interviews, and analysis of hard data. Summary findings are presented, along with recommendations for addressing areas in need of change.

88. Cullen, D. "Career Barriers: Do We Need More Research?" *Women in Management Research Symposium*, Mount Saint Vincent University, Nova Scotia, 1988, pp. 3.28-3.36.

Documents the study of career barriers for women as having focused on the individual behavior and struggle of women, and not on organizational structures in which they operate. Argues that future research on career barriers should focus on the characteristics of organizations, rather than on the characteristics that women need to succeed. A selective overview of the "individualist approach" to career barriers is given, and some of its limits are explored.

89. Dipboye, R.L. "Problems and Progress of Women in Management." *Working Women: Past, Present, Future*, ed. Koziara, K.S., Moskow, M.H., and Tanner, L.D. Washington: *Bureau of National Affairs*, 1987: pp. 118-153.

Holds that the status of women in management has improved dramatically over the past two decades, yet management is still a "male domain." Argues that the barriers still exist for women, and that they have become more complex and subtle. Sex-stereotyping is a "primary roadblock" and women who aspire to managerial careers may encounter barriers from "gate-keepers" (e.g., personnel offices, recruiters, instruments used to assess managerial talent). Further, once hired, women face other barriers that limit their advancement (e.g., exclusion from male networks, bias in job assignments and performance evaluation, lack of mentors, inequitable compensation, sexual harassment and conflicts between work and family roles). Little hope is offered for immediate change, but strategies and remedies to reduce these barriers are given.

90. Federally Employed Women. *Report of a Survey on Women and the Federal Women's Program in the Federal Government.* Washington: Federally Employed Women, Inc., 1991.

Using survey results from 22 agencies and departments, analyzes problems and barriers women in the federal government face. Finds that women continue to hold disproportionately more lower-level jobs than men (i.e., they are concentrated in the clerical occupations and at grade levels 1 through 8); complaints of sex discrimination are still pervasive, and the Federal Women's Program (FWP) has received limited management and budgetary support from most organizations. Argues that in order to meet the mandates of the FWP, the Office of Personnel Management must take an aggressive leadership role, and FWP Managers must work full-time, not collaterally, to overcome the lack of progress the program has made to date.

91. Forbes, J. Benjamin. "Women Executives: Breaking Down Barriers?" *Business Horizons.* 31 (November/December 1988): 6-9.

Analyzes the current placement and distribution of women with respect to position, industry, age, education, and geography. Compares the state of women's position in 1982 to 1987.

92. Fraker, S. "Why Women Aren't Getting To the Top." *Fortune*, Vol. 109, No. 8, April 16, 1984: pp. 40-45.

Argues that subtle barriers exist that still preclude women from making it to top management ranks. Some identified include: "comfort level" with female managers, giving the best assignments to men, not giving women managers the same kind of constructive criticism that men receive, perceived management style of women, and the assumption that women with children are not free to take on special tasks or travel. Examines the issue of "critical mass," and documents studies which have shown that even though resistance to women in management drops quickly after the first few women enter the ranks, it seems to resurface as the number of women managers reaches 15%. Recommendations are made about what employers can do to open the executive ranks to women (e.g., flexibility, revised personnel policies, rewarding managers for developing talent and vigilantly supervising the hiring and promotion process).

93. Friedman, D.E. "Why the Glass Ceiling?" *Across the Board*, July-August 1988, pp. 33-37.

Examines barriers women face in moving up within organizations, and discusses in particular the difficulties of reconciling competing work and family needs. Asserts that previous analyses of women's relatively slow progress have "overlooked, underestimated and misinterpreted family factors," and argues that employers should do more for both male and female employees in the way of developing policies and work environments that are supportive of family needs. Some examples of such policies are given.

94. Hardesty, Sarah, and Nehama Jacobs. *Success and Betrayal: The Crisis of Women in Corporate America*. Watts, Franklin, 1986.

Two women executives challenge previous assumptions about how far women will rise and the value of the rewards bestowed on women in the workforce. Discusses barriers women encounter and the effect of the "hidden agenda women bring to corporate life."

95. James, Chuck. "Women in the Forest Service: The Early Years." *Journal of Forestry*. 89 (March 1991): 14-17.

Gives a brief account of the first women who worked for the United States Forest Service and the barriers they faced.

96. Kanter, Rosabeth Moss. *Men and Women of the Corporation*. New York: Basic Books, 1977.

Classic organization development work which outlines cultural and environmental elements in organizations which serve as barriers to the success of women in organizations. Sets forth the notion of "tokenism" and the negative effect this phenomenon has on the advancement of women in corporate America. Argues that when structural barriers are eliminated and opportunity is controlled men and women will succeed at the same rate.

97. Kanter, Rosabeth Moss. "Men and Women of the Corporation Revisited." *Management Review*. 76 (No. 3, 1987): 14-16.

Reevaluates the hypotheses of the 1977 book *Men and Women of the Corporation* (see entry 96) in which it was argued that differences in the behavior and success of women and men had more to do with what the organization did to them than with inherent differences in ability or ambition. The 1977 book concluded that when men and women were dealt a "similar hand," and given similar places in the corporate game, they behaved in similar ways. The problem lay in the fact that men and women were rarely dealt a similar hand. Ten years after the original hypothesis, Kanter sees progress for women. Areas where there has been improvement and as well as new and unique problems that have surfaced for women are discussed.

98. Kennedy, R. Bryan. "Recruitment: Preference for Veterans May Impede Women." *Personnel Journal*. 69 (September 1990): 124,126.

Outlines the claim that the U.S. government's programs aimed at hiring women may be undermined by preferential hiring practices established for veterans. Cites the Veterans' Preference Act of 1944, which ensures higher retention standing for veterans in case of workforce reductions, and the Veteran's Readjustment Program (VRP) which provides for direct recruitment of Vietnam-era veterans as bypassing traditional U.S. Office of Personnel Management recruitment procedures. Further, cites The Civil Service Reform Act of 1978 which provided for noncompetitive recruitment of "30% disabled veterans." Asserts that these policies directly conflict with the policies of Equal Employment Opportunity. Argues that veterans' preference will continue to be a barrier to recruitment to all non-veterans, and since military service has traditionally been a male domain, veterans' preference will most severely affect women.

99. Lewis, Gregory B., and Meesung Ha. "Impact of the Baby Boom on Career Success in Federal Civil Service." *Public Administration Review*. 48 (November/December 1988): 951-956.

Examines the question of the "employment bulge" (i.e., large numbers of federal employees aged 35 to 44), and raises questions about the effect it will have on the career prospects of younger federal employees. Compares personnel records for 1976 and 1986, and concludes that most federal employees in 1986 were doing as well as or better than employees of the same age in 1976. Men aged 25 to 39, however, held lower grades than men of the same age a decade before. Data show women progressing at all age levels, but still trailing men. Argues that the baby boom may serve to decrease the likelihood of holding a supervisory position.

100. Markham, William T., Patrick O. Macken, Charles M. Bonjean, and Judy A. Corder. "A Note on Sex, Geographic Mobility, and Career Advancement." *Social Forces*. 61 (No. 4, 1983): 1138-1146.

Using data from interviews with 32 managers within 6 offices of a federal agency, and questionnaire results from 897 employees and supervisors, investigates the notion that with increasing career aspirations among women and greater prevalence of dual-career marriages, sex differences in geographic mobility for occupational advancement are one barrier to women's career advancement. Historically, geographic mobility has been virtually an occupational requirement for managers, and it may have helped many acquire supervisory positions. Differences in mobility and willingness to move between men and women appear as expected. Although not strikingly large, they were big enough to be noticed by managers sensitive to the issue.

101. Martin, Lynn. *A Report on the Glass Ceiling Initiative*. Washington: U.S. Department of Labor, 1991.

Report by Secretary of Labor, Lynn Martin on the phenomenon termed "glass ceiling" which is defined as "those artificial barriers based on attitudinal or organizational bias that prevent qualified individuals from advancing upward in their organization into management-level positions." Based on a study of nine Fortune 500 companies, identifies some of the barriers contributing to the "glass ceiling." These include recruitment practices that rely on informal networks--from which women are often excluded, and executive search firms where affirmative action/EEO requirements were not made known.

102. Martin, P., D. Harrison, and D. Dinitto. "Advancement by Women in Hierarchial Organizations: A Multilevel Analysis of Problems and Prospects." *The Journal of Applied Behavioral Science*. 19 (No. 1, 1983): 19-33.

Examines problems related to women's advancement in hierarchial organizations within a five-level framework of social organization: societal, institutional, organizational, role, and individual. Identifies two major problems women face for each of the five levels, and gives possible solutions. Concludes that meaningful change in women's status in hierarchical organizations requires efforts on all five levels of social organization. Also concludes that division of labor between men and women related to work and family responsibilities must change before women can receive equitable treatment in the workplace.

103. Moore, L.L., ed. *Not As Far As You Think*. Lexington, MA: Lexington Books, 1986.

Discusses psychological barriers and external barriers women face on the job, and offers solutions for overcoming these barriers. Argues that since barriers are internal (i.e., psychological) and external, individuals must change as well as organizations.

104. Morrison, Ann M., Randall P. White, and Ellen Van Velsor. *Breaking the Glass Ceiling*. Reading, MA: Addison-Wesley, Inc., 1987.

Defines the "glass ceiling" as not just a barrier to advancement which is based on an individual's inability to handle a higher-level job; but rather the "glass ceiling" applies to women as a group who are kept from advancing simply because they are women. Describes how some women have accomplished the feat of breaking through the glass ceiling, and provides practical advice for others who want to do the same.

105. Nodell, Bobbi. "Women in government." *Government Executive*. 20 (August 1988): 10-57.

Reports on the progress of women into the executive levels of the federal civil service. Profiles several successful women in government who "broke the glass ceiling," and gives statistics about the "typical" female senior executive. Reports on results of a survey sent to alumni of the Federal Executive Institute which shows that women are less optimistic than men about their prospects for further advancement; yet 73 percent of women, compared with 64 percent of men are satisfied with working for the federal government. Also gives advice for how to deal with barriers to advancement, including information on professional networks.

106. Ospina, Sonia. Opportunity and Satisfaction: A Structural Approach to the Study of Work Attitudes. State University of New York at Stony Brook, Ph.D diss., 1989.

Studies three occupational groups of employees in public organizations, clerks, analysts and operators, to ascertain if structural differences in opportunity affect satisfaction. Confirms that employees in career ladders with the best opportunities are most satisfied. Challenges the notion that job satisfaction is based on psychological and environmental models. Concludes that structural reward and opportunity related to promotion, compensation, and personal growth are salient factors, and attention should be focused more on structural issues than on the more traditional explanations like personal orientations or isolated job conditions.

107. Pickering, Tonya H., and Brian H. Kleiner. "Women: Power and Advancement." *Equal Opportunities International,* 8 (No. 3, 1989): 24-27.

Argues that women have had a difficult time breaking into management ranks because of cultural factors, but also because of problems women themselves perpetuate. Factors necessary to achieve organizational power are discussed, including knowledge and competence, image, personality, and personal life.

108. Povall, M. "Overcoming Barriers to Women's Advancement in European Organizations." *Personnel Review.* 13 (No. 1, 1984): 32-40.

Discusses organizational and institutional patterns, practices, rules, and norms which inhibit and thwart women entering and advancing in organizations. These patterns and practices are linked to personnel policies and processes (organizational factors) as well as job and career-ladder definition (structural factors).

109. Redclift, Nanneke, and Thea M. Sinclair. *Working Women: International Perspectives on Labour and Gender Ideology.* Routledge, 1991.

Discusses cultural and economic elements that create disadvantages for women in the workplace. Covers an eclectic selection of environments including library work, women in retailing, Turkish women factory workers, personal strategy and public participation in Egypt, a mining community in Kent, England, women shop stewards in Great Britain, and Greek women's cooperatives.

110. Rexford, Stephen J., and Lisa A. Mainiero. "The 'Right Stuff' of Management: Challenges Confronting Women." *SAM Advanced Management Journal.* 51 (Spring 1986): 36-40.

Discusses subtle cultural barriers that exist for women trying to break into top positions. Advises women to use their strengths in consensus building, participatory decision-making, and cooperation to replace the male-dominated and male-oriented management style and system of the past. Urges women to develop their political skills and offers several guidelines for becoming action-oriented, and culturally and politically aware and astute.

111. Solomon, Charlene Marmer. "Careers Under Glass." *Personnel Journal.* 69 (No. 4, 1990): 96-101.

Examines the private sector's record on opportunities afforded to women. States that only 2% of top executives in Corporate America are women and that female vice presidents earn 42% less than men in the same jobs. Cites Corning and Honeywell as model employers who are working to break the "glass ceiling."

112. Spruell, G. "Making It, Big Time--Is it Really Tougher for Women?" *Training and Development Journal*, August 1985: 30-33.

Discusses two relatively dichotomous views of the advancement (or lack thereof) of women. The first argues that the reasons that women have not advanced like men are related to individual behavior and beliefs of women themselves. Several possible causes are entertained: women do not have high enough aspirations to achieve; they don't choose the "right" jobs (e.g., staff versus line jobs); they haven't been part of the labor force long enough to obtain high-level jobs; and women are not organized enough to achieve family and career balance. The second argument, discussed by those who support more formal equal employment opportunity for women, cites subtle barriers facing women such as cultural views of appropriate work behavior, women's lack of visibility in organizations, and the difficulty of reconciling family and career.

113. Steinberg, Ronnie J., Lois Haignere, and Cynthia Chertos. "Managerial Promotions in the Public Sector: The Impact of Eligibility Requirements on Women and Minorities." *Work and Occupations*. 17 (August 1990): 284-301.

Analyzes barriers to the promotion of women and minorities into managerial positions in the New York State government work force using data from those promoted through a formal examination process and those promoted through nonexamination or administrative transfer. Refutes the commonly believed theory that competitive examination processes and the "Rule of Three" selection procedure create barriers to advancement for women. Concludes that the main barrier to promotion of women and minorities is in meeting eligibility requirements.

114. Task Force on Barriers to Women in the Public Service. *Beneath the Veneer : The Report of the Task Force on Barriers to Women in the Public Service.* Ottawa, Canada: Ministry of Supply and Services Canada, 1990.

Reports on barriers that women face in the Canadian civil service. Analyzes numbers/representation of women in higher echelon jobs, and outlines barriers they faced during advancement. Also includes interviews with successful women who reported on both subtle, intangible barriers as well as formal, structural barriers. Concludes with recommendations for improving the status of women in the Canadian civil service.

115. U.S. General Accounting Office. *Conflicting Congressional Policies: Veterans' Preference and Apportionment vs. Equal Employment Opportunity; Report to the Congress by the Comptroller General of the United States.* Washington: G.A.O., 1977.

Analyzes the effects of veterans' preference and apportionment on the opportunities women have to compete for entry-level employment in the federal civil service. This is contrasted with the responsibility federal agencies have to hire women in order to accomplish affirmative action goals.

116. U.S. General Accounting Office. *Reduction in Force Can Sometimes Be More Costly to Agencies Than Attrition and Furlough; Report to the Director, Office of Management and Budget, July 24, 1985.* Washington: G.A.O., 1985.

Analyzes the costs of eight Reductions in Force (RIF's). Assesses levels of downgrading that resulted from these RIF's, and the general effects on the employment status of women and minorities.

117. U.S. Merit Systems Protection Board. *A Question of Equity: Women and the Glass Ceiling in the Federal Government.* Washington: G.P.O., 1992.

Using data from the Central Personnel Data File as well as focus group and survey data, issues of barriers to advancement of women in the federal civil service are explored. Results demonstrate that women face subtle cultural barriers in the form of stereotypes, and negative assumptions about their effectiveness and their commitment. Also concludes that women are not promoted less than men at the higher levels (i.e., GS/GM-13) but rather at the lower levels, specifically the GS-9 and GS-11 levels. This results in a paucity of women in the "pipeline" to reach the higher organizational levels. Recommendations such as a renewed commitment to agency equal employment opportunity, evaluation of all the criteria being used to assess potential for advancement, systematic eradication of gender-based stereotypes and assessments of barriers for women within agencies, as well as women taking advantage of all possible developmental programs available are set forth.

118. Vertz, Laura L. "Women, Occupational Advancement, and Mentoring: An Analysis of One Public Organization." *Public Administration Review.* 45 (May/June 1985): 415-423.

Offers a case study of the Milwaukee District Office of the Internal Revenue Service to illustrate barriers women face in advancement. Argues that mentoring is a useful tool for women who want to advance, but cautions that the special problems women face in organizations must be factored in and dealt with in the mentoring process. A five-step approach to accomplish this is provided.

119. ---. "Symposium: Reduction-in-Force Policy; Issues and Perspectives. *Public Administration Quarterly.* 10 (Spring 1986): 3-109.

Contents: "The Political Context of a Reduction-In-Force Policy: On the Misunderstanding of an Important Phenomenon," by Wilbur C. Rich; "Attitudes of Senior Personnel Officials and Employees Toward RIF Policies," by Cynthia Shaughnessy; "Managerial Implications of Reduction-In-Force," by N. Joseph Cayer; "Impacts of Privatization Upon Career Public Employees," by William M. Timmins; "Caveat Public Employer: Selected Legal Issues in Non-Federal Agency Reductions-In-Force," by Robert L. Spurrier, Jr.; "Workforce Reduction and Productivity," by Marc Holzer; "Minority, Women, and Civil Service Reform: Seven Years Later," by Lawrence C. Howard.

SEX SEGREGATION

120. Baron, James N., and W. Beilby. "Organizational Barriers to Gender Equality: Sex Segregation of Jobs and Opportunities." In Rossi, A.S., *Gender and the Life Course*. New York: Aldine Publishing Company, 1988

Demonstrates the persistence of gender stratification in the U.S. economy, and suggests that firms differ less in the extent of sex segregation than in the organizational structures and processes in place which create and maintain sex segregation in the workplace. Implications of segregation for the careers of men and women are examined, and policies and strategies aimed at achieving equity are discussed. Concludes that sex segregation will continue unless and until employers adopt proactive policies to reverse past trends.

121. Bergmann, Barbara R. *The Economic Emergence of Women*. New York: Basic Books Inc., 1986.

Documents the "economic revolution" that has occurred as women have entered the workforce, and discusses the barriers that women face in today's labor market. Argues that the "root" of the disadvantages that women face stem from sex segregation on the job. Various reasons for sex discrimination are discussed, as well as the forms that discrimination takes, and its consequences. Concludes that government policy is needed; a twelve-point agenda for action is proposed.

122. Gutek, Barbara A. "Sex Segregation and Women at Work: A Selective Review." *Applied Psychology: An International Review.* 37 (No. 2, 1988): 103-120.

Reviews the body of literature that covers several subjects related to problems women face in the workplace. Topics include: sex-role spillover (the carry-over of expectations about sex roles to the job), short career ladders, tokenism and its implications. Sex-segregation of work is a common theme throughout.

123. Reskin, Barbara., and Hartmann, H. *Women's Work, Men's Work-- Sex Segregation on the Job.* Washington: National Academy Press, 1986.

Report by the Committee on Women's Employment and Related Issues reviews evidence of sex segregation and its negative consequences for women and for society. Attempts to explain concentrations of women in "lower status" jobs that pay less, and options for improving women's job opportunities. Argues that cultural factors and societal beliefs about gender and work significantly contribute to the employment status of women, and that commitment to equal opportunity is one factor that is crucial for advancing women's employment opportunities. Recommendations for improvement center on enforcement of equal opportunity laws as well as improvement of education.

STEREOTYPES

124. Chusmir, Leonard H., and Douglas E. Durand. "The Female Factor." *Training and Development Journal*. 41 (August 1987): 32-37.

Argues that stereotypes and myths about female employees cause many organizations to under-utilize women. Attempts to refute some of the most commonly held stereotypes (e.g., women's high rate of absenteeism, lack of commitment to their jobs, etc.). Gives advice to managers on strategies to help women succeed in organizations.

125. Colwill, Nina L. "Fear of Success in Women: Organizational Reality or Psychological Mythology?" *Business Quarterly*. 49 (Fall 1984): 20-21.

Revisits Horner's (1968) concept of "fear of success" in women and the research that followed. Argues that Horner's conclusions are fallacious.

126. Epstein, C. *Deceptive Distinctions: Sex, Gender and the Social Order*. New Haven: Yale University Press.

Focuses on the changing roles of men and women in society over the last twenty years. Argues that stereotypes about differences between men and women are more superficial than society has dictated. Current theories are reviewed--socialization theory, the human capitol theory, social structural analysis and theories of discrimination--in an effort to explain the sexual division of labor. Argues that the causes of occupational segregation are found in a "combination of factors such as employee discrimination, women's choices, family pressures and public policy." Subtle barriers for women in the hiring and promotion processes are also discussed, and the importance of networks, mentors and access to those with power are highlighted.

127. Johnson, A. "Women Managers: Old Stereotypes Die Hard." *Management Review*, December 1987: pp.31-42.

Examines barriers female managers face in the workplace, including the "old boy" network, myths about women's goals and abilities, sex-segregated workplaces and absence of long-term goals by women. Gives recommendations about how informal and unstructured barriers that exist within and outside organizations can be broken down. Also cites examples of several successful employers in recruiting, retaining and developing female managers. Argues that employers must change their attitudes and the organizational structures in which they operate before discrimination in the hiring and promotion of women can be eradicated.

128. Pearson, Dick. "Perceptions About Women Managers." *Supervisory Management*. 29 (October 1984): 29-34.

Discusses general management reluctance to promote women into higher-level jobs because of erroneous perceptions about women's inability to make decisions, and some people's belief that women will take jobs away from men. True barriers to women entering management ranks, it is argued, center on the fact that women have children, and employers believe that they will be more likely to leave their jobs to be mothers.

129. Peder, M., and R. Fritchie. "Training Men to Work With Women." *Women in Management Review*, vol. 1, no. 2, 1985: pp. 75-84.

Argues that traditional approaches which deal with improving the number and quality of women managers are misplaced. Maintains that instead of concentrating on defining and analyzing barriers to women's advancement, the critical issues have been forgotten. Those critical issues relate to people's feelings, values and attitudes. Concludes that until these are addressed, real and permanent change will not happen.

130. Ruble, T., R. Cohen, and D. Ruble. "Sex Stereotypes--Occupational Barriers for Women." *American Behavioral Scientist*, vol. 27, no. 3, January/February 1984: pp. 339-356.

Reviews current literature and concludes that sex-stereotypes and occupational sex-segregation reinforce each other and serve to create different barriers for women at different points in their careers. Women tend to fall prey to these phenomena when they make choices about which occupational fields to enter and at promotion and advancement stages when organizations practice bias based on stereotypes. Also concludes that biases are especially pronounced when information about performance is vague.

CHAPTER 3

Affirmative Action & Equal Employment Opportunity

"No person should be denied equal rights because of the shape of her skin." Pat Paulson.

GENERAL

131. Beck, Ann C., and Mary K. Stohr-Gillmore. "Gender and Harassment Victim Support for Affirmative Action. *State and Local Government Review.* 23 (Winter 1991): 31-36.

Using data from a 1987 survey in a county government in Washington State, concludes that women who consider themselves victims of sexual harassment make up a large source from which high levels of support for more active affirmative action efforts stem. Using an analysis of demographic trends, it is also argued that a gender gap in support for affirmative action has developed.

132. Coyle, A. "The Limits of Change: Local Government and Equal Opportunities for Women." *Public Administration.* 67 (No. 1, 1988): 39-50.

Examines equal opportunity policies related to women adopted by local governments in Great Britain from 1982 to 1987. Women in

British local governments are concentrated in low-paid, low-status jobs and under-represented as decision-makers even in those departments where women are in the majority. Concludes that equal opportunity policies have achieved limited results. Argues that policies have failed because of few invested resources, little managerial or political support and guidance, and no implementation mechanisms or management accountability. Concludes that "collective, organizational and structural change" must be developed in order that "new organizational structures, new cultures and new values" can emerge.

133. DeVries, Christine M. "The Advancement of Women in the Federal Government: A Progress Report." Washington: *Federally Employed Women*, 1987.

Discusses progress made by women employed by the federal government. Outlines the various issues federally employed women have fought for including adequate child care facilities, upward mobility programs, funding for agencies charged with ensuring non-discrimination, flexible work schedules, and fair wages. Argues that women are slowly moving into upper management and traditionally-male occupations.

134. DiPrete, Thomas A., and Whitman T. Soule. "Gender and Promotion in Segmented Job Ladder Systems." *American Sociological Review*. 53 (February 1988): 26-40.

Discusses gender differences in promotion rates among federal civil service employees during the 1970's. Although no gender differences appeared in the higher grades, and no "zero-order" difference existed in the lower grades, concludes that the greatest disadvantage for women was near the boundary between the lower- and upper-level grades.

*   DiPrete, Thomas A. "The Professionalization of Administration and Equal Employment Opportunity in the U.S. Federal Government." Cited above as item 10.

135. Fagenson, Ellen A. "Women's Work Orientation: Something Old, Something New." *Group and Organization Studies*. 11 (March-June 1986): 75-100.

Tests two theories about why women are disproportionately represented in lower-level jobs. The individual-centered perspective argues that women's orientations, behavior, and attitudes are contrary to that which is essential for senior management jobs. The organization centered view argues that the individual's position in the hierarchy will shape her or his attitudes. Using survey data administered to women attending a conference on business in New York City, the author concludes that the organization-centered approach is more supportable than the individual-centered perspective.

136. Ferguson, K.E. *The Feminist Case Against Bureaucracy*. Series Women in the Political Economy, ed., R.J. Steinberg. Philadelphia: Temple University Press, 1984.

Feminist book which argues that political resistance is a viable route to creating opposition to inequity. Clarifies structures and processes of power in bureaucratic societies and discusses their effects on individuals. Concludes that there should be a non-bureaucratic approach to solving problems that organizations create for women.

137. Heilman, M.E., and J.M. Herlihy. "Affirmative Action, Negative Reaction? Some Moderating Conditions." *Organizational Behavior and Human Performance*. 33 (1984): 204-213.

Summarizes a study done on male and female college-bound high school students and discusses the implications of the findings for affirmative action programs. Discusses the theory of increasing the number of women role models in traditionally male-dominated occupations. Argues that the way in which women obtain jobs is crucial, and it influences the interest women have in these jobs. Results from the study discussed show that it is important to explain the process by which larger numbers of women are placed in occupations that were in the past reserved for men, since men tend to assume that women are placed in these jobs because of factors other than merit. Women, on the other hand, assume that female incumbents are hired on the basis of merit.

138. Kingsley, J. Donald. *Representative Bureaucracy: An Interpretation of the British Civil Service.* Yellow Springs, OH: Antioch Press, 1944.

Seminal work in "representative bureaucracy." Kingsley said, "The democratic state cannot afford to exclude and considerable body of its citizens from full participation in its affairs...in a democracy competence alone is not enough. The public service must also be representative if the State is to liberate rather than to enslave."

139. Kranz, Harry. *The Participatory Democracy, Women and Minorities in a More Representative Public Service.* Lexington, MA: Lexington Books, D.C. Heath and Company, 1976.

Examines the development of the bureaucracy; analyzes some of its problems and presents alternatives for change. Contends that bureaucracy is not representative of the general population, and has historically operated to exclude minorities and women from participation. Substantial statistical evidence is presented to support this claim, and insights and recommendations are offered for addressing concerns raised.

140. Krislov, Samuel. *Representative Bureaucracy.* Englewood Cliffs, NJ: Prentice-Hall, 1974.

Classic work in American public administration which argues that the meritocracy must be responsive and accountable to any democratic society. This includes demographic representation of the social structure at large.

141. Krislov, Samuel, and David H. Rosenbloom. *Representative Bureaucracy and the American Political System.* New York: Praeger, 1981.

Update of Krislov's (1974) previous work (see item 140) which furthers the argument that representativeness of the democracy's civil service is paramount on several levels. Issues of representation in personnel, perspective, and societal position are discussed. Concludes that revitalization of the federal service will require a strengthening of representativeness and quality, which must go hand-in-hand.

142. Luneburg, William V. "The Federal Personnel Complaint, Appeal, and Grievance Systems: A Structural Overview and Proposed Revisions." *Kentucky Law Journal.* 78 (No. 1, 1989): 1-128.

Relates EEO processes before and after passage of the Civil Service Reform Act (CSRA) of 1978. Outlines issues related to structural and organizational changes as a result of CSRA focusing on the merit system, the EEOC, the negotiated grievance process, and the Federal Labor Relations Authority.

143. Meier, Kenneth J. "Constraints on Affirmative Action." *Policy Studies Journal.* 7 (Winter 1978): 208-213.

Outlines social and Political barriers which thwart full acceptance and implementation of Affirmative Action policies. Structural as well as environmental factors are discussed, and recommendations for improvement are set forth.

144. Meier, Kenneth J. "Representative Bureaucracy: An Empirical Analysis." *American Political Science Review.* 69 (June 1975): 526-542.

An analysis and empirical test of the theory and existence of "representative bureaucracy" in the United States. Outlines weaknesses in the theory by critically examining its basic premises, and concludes that in fact representative bureaucracy does not exist.

145. Nachmias, David, and David H. Rosenbloom. "Measuring Bureaucratic Representation and Integration." *Public Administration Review*. 33 (November/December 1973): 590-597.

Introduced the "measure of variation" (MV) to determine demographic representativeness within federal agencies. MV is determined by using a ratio of the number of demographic differences that are present related to the number of demographic differences that are possible. The higher the MV score of an organization, the closer it is to integration, and thus representation. Used mostly in representation of minorities in organizations, but may be applied to representation of women as well.

146. Paton, A. *Women in Management: Affirmative Action and Merit in the Federal Public Service*. Masters Research Project, School of Public Administration, Queen's University (Canada), 1985.

Discusses potential contradiction between affirmative action programs and merit principles. Argues that the merit principle has produced a homogeneous civil service and further draws a distinction between merit principles and the merit system. Contends that access to training and other "non-competitive" advantages that have been denied to women in the past might enhance their competitiveness for promotions. Concludes that "merit" may be an evolving concept, as the idea of a representative civil service may be an important part of the working definition of any merit system.

147. President's Commission on the Status of Women. *Report of the Committee on Federal Employment.* Washington: G.P.O., 1963.

Report of President Kennedy's Commission, which was headed by Eleanor Roosevelt, on the status of the employment of women in the federal service. Found that discriminatory selection and promotion practices existed, and set forth recommendations (many of which were subsequently adopted) to remedy problems identified.

148. Rosenbloom, David H. *Federal Equal Employment Opportunity: Politics and Public Personnel Administration.* New York: Praeger, 1977.

Outlines history or equal employment opportunity law in the federal sector. Discourse pre-dates the Civil Service Reform Act (1978). Issues of competing goals and demands are articulated with a focus on the merit system, goals and timetables, and the Politics of implementing EEO and Affirmative Action.

149. Sigelman, Lee. "Organizational Regeneration and Political Change: a Model with Applications to Affirmative Action." *American Journal of Political Science.* 30 (February 1986): 79-107.

Develops a model of organizational regeneration. This process is defined as the way organizations renew and reconfigure themselves as there is attrition and retirement. Argues that the regeneration process is full of political implications. The model presented is developed using employment of women in state and local governments.

150. Tell, David. "Women's History and EEOC v. Sears: Differences and Inequality." *Society.* 24 (September/October 1987): 10-16.

An interview with Alice Kessler-Harris, an historian who testified on behalf of the Equal Employment Opportunity Commission in its sex discrimination suit against Sears, Roebuck and Company. Focuses on Kessler-Harris's role in the trial, as well as general themes of sex discrimination in employment, women and labor, and affirmative action.

151. United States Congress. House. Committee on Education and Labor. Subcommittee on Employment Opportunities. *Joint Oversight Hearing on the Federal Equal Employment Opportunity Complaint Process. Joint Hearing Before the Subcommittee on Employment Opportunities of the Committee on Education and Labor and the Subcommittee on Civil Service of the Committee on Post Office and Civil Service, House of Representatives*. 101st Cong., 2nd sess. 1990. Serial No. 101-117.

Hearing on the EEO complaint process. Purpose is to gather information on whether the process fails or succeeds in its mission to guarantee a discrimination-free workplace.

152. U.S. Department of the Interior. *Profile of Women at Work in the U.S. Department of the Interior*. Washington: U.S. Department of the Interior, 1990.

Highlights the significant contributions and achievements of a selected group of exemplary women from diverse occupations. Women were selected for inclusion on the basis of their accomplishments made toward the advancement of the Department's mission and/or improvement of the work environment, either as part of their official duties or as volunteers.

153. U.S. General Accounting Office. *Information on Internal EEO Activities at Selected Federal Agencies, June 14, 1985*. Washington: G.A.O., 1985.

154. Vertz, Laura L. "Gender-Based Job Status in the Federal Bureaucracy: An Integration of Situational, Structural, Socialization, and Personality Explanations." Ph.D. diss., The University of Wisconsin-Milwaukee, 1983.

Outlines the issue of gender-based job status using survey data from the Milwaukee District Office of the Internal Revenue Service, and relates job status issues to "representative bureaucracy." Factors like personality attributes, gender role attitudes, domestic constraints, and structural constraints are synthesized into a single model to explain gender-based job status. Implications for equal employment opportunity policy are discussed.

155. Washington Council of Lawyers. *Report of the Washington Council of Lawyers on the Federal EEO Administrative Process*. Washington: The Council, 1987.

Reports results of a study of the operation of the administrative EEO process in the federal government using data from four federal agencies: the Department of Agriculture, Health and Human Services, the Postal Service, and the Veterans Administration. Focuses on three aspects of the administration of the EEO process: speed with which claims are processed, the even-handedness with which agency EEO staff handle claims, and the extent to which agency EEO staff possess the skills and knowledge to perform EEO duties.

156. Wurster, Barbara C. "Women in the Higher Public Service: Recruitment and Careers." *Equal Opportunities International* (UK). 10 (No. 2, 1991): 19-27.

In 1987, a Steering Committee on Women in the Higher Public Services was established at the European Institute of Public Administration (EIPA). In 1989, this committee studied the issue of recruitment and career planning. Findings included: 1) target figures for female recruitment are fixed only in the Netherlands and in the European

Commission, and 2) it no longer is a lack of qualifications that hinders women from being promoted. Recommends flexible models to help female personnel combine family responsibilities with work responsibilities.

REPRESENTATION OF WOMEN IN THE WORKFORCE

157. Aron, Cindy S. "To Barter Their Souls for Gold": Female Clerks in Federal Government Offices, 1862-1890." *Journal of American History*. 67 (March 1981): 835-853.

Examines the status of women in clerical positions in the Federal Government during the latter part of the nineteenth century. Details the history of the entrance of women into clerical positions in the federal service starting in 1862, and argues that this opened a new field of female employment. By the early 1890's women held 5,600 of the nearly 17,600 positions in the executive departments in Washington, and at the turn of the century over 104,000 women comprised 29 percent of the office workers in the United States. One of the major reasons the government decided to allow women into the workforce was because they commanded much lower salaries than their male clerical counterparts. As time passed, however, these women found it necessary to acquire not only new skills, but new goals and attitudes as well. In the process they began to convince society, and themselves, that Victorian ladies could be successfully transformed into working women.

158. Aron, Cindy S. *Ladies and Gentlemen of the Civil Service*. New York: Oxford University Press, 1987.

Details the history of the influx of women into the federal civil service. Asserts that the "experiment" of bringing women into the workforce in the 19th century was started in the federal civil service, and had a profound effect on how we define our middle class today. Discusses why the government decided to employ women and how that decision was implemented. Argues that women influenced the nature and organization of work in the federal government and were able to succeed more than in other spheres of employment.

159. Benimadhu, Prem P., and Ruth Wright. "Employment Equity: Impact of the Legislation. *Canadian Business Review*. 18 (Summer 1991): 22-25.

Using data from a 1990 survey of 365 federally regulated organizations covered under the Employment Equity Act (Canada), examines changes in the recruitment and promotion of women and minorities.

160. Dometrius, Nelson C. "Minorities and Women Among State Agency Leaders." *Social Science Quarterly*. 65 (March 1984): 127-137.

Identifies trends in female and minority representation in state agency leadership using 1974 and 1978 EEOC and American State Administrator Project data. Salary comparisons show that women and minorities are not as well represented in high-level positions and their progress since the passage of the EEO Act has been slow. Some occupational link is determined, as representation varies by functional area.

161. Fasman, Zachary. "Affirmative Action Receives Green Light from Divided Court." *Legal Times*. 9 (May 25, 1987): 12-14.

Analyzes two supreme court cases, United States v. Paradise and Johnson v. Santa Clara County Transportation Agency. Discusses the issue of "reverse discrimination" in the context of these cases, and the resulting implications. Summarizes the significance of the supreme court's decisions to affirm the use of voluntary affirmative action plans and the constitutionality of "court-ordered numerical relief in employment discrimination cases."

162. Hale, Mary M., and Rita Mae Kelly, editors. *Gender, Bureaucracy, and Democracy: Careers and Equal Opportunity in the Public Sector.* New York: Greenwood Press, 1989.

Looks at the status of women in several state governments-- Arizona, Texas, Utah, and California. Examines the careers of successful women, and the obstacles with which they have had to deal. Concludes with recommendations for the future vis-a-vis equal employment opportunity.

163. Jost, Kenneth. "The Women at Justice: Meese Was Part of the Problem. Is Thornburgh the Solution?" *American Bar Association Journal.* 75 (August 1989): 54-60.

Comments on some female lawyers' experience at the Department of Justice. Argues that, despite official statements for equal opportunities for women, many lawyers inside and outside the department feel that Justice has not institutionalized policies to meet affirmative action goals.

164. Kellough, J. Edward, and Susan Ann Kay. "Affirmative Action in the Federal Bureaucracy: An Impact Assessment." *Review of Public Personnel Administration.* 6 (Spring 1986): 1-13.

Analyzes the effects of affirmative action programs in the federal government by comparing pre- and post-policy data from the Civil Service Commission and the Equal Employment Opportunity Commission. Concludes that affirmative action programs did not have a big impact on the employment of blacks; these programs were somewhat more effective for women.

165. Kellough, J. Edward. "Federal Agencies and Affirmative Action for Blacks and Women." *Social Science Quarterly.* 71 (March 1990): 83-92.

Reports employment progress of blacks and women in the 22 largest federal agencies following the 1971 authorization of numerical goals and timetables in agency Affirmative Action plans. Focuses on employment in middle- and higher-level positions. Develops an index ranking the agencies studied based on the extent to which they improved their EEO performance.

166. Kellough, J. Edward. "Integration in the Public Workplace: Determinants of Minority and Female Employment in Federal Agencies. *Public Administration Review.* 50 (September/October 1990): 557-566.

Examines employment trends of minorities and women in federal agencies as of September, 1988. Concentrates on factors that influence integration of women and minorities into federal agencies. Some factors discovered include agency size, union strength, blue collar/clerical employment, and the rate of new hires. Concludes that "contextual variables" explain a lot of the variation in the integration of federal agencies.

167. Kellough, J. Edward. "The 1978 Civil Service Reform and Federal Equal Employment Opportunity." *American Review of Public Administration.* 19 (December 1989): 313-324.

Examines employment trends of blacks and women in middle- and higher-level positions and looks for possible influences of elements of the 1978 Civil Service Reform Act (CSRA) designed to advance Equal Employment Opportunity in the federal civil service. Concludes that long-term employment trends for women in the middle-level grades appear unchanged following CSRA, and the employment rate in higher grades increased following the CSRA.

168. Lewis, Gregory B. "Progress Toward Racial and Sexual Equality in the Federal Civil Service?" *Public Administration Review.* 48 (May-June 1988): 700-707.

Using federal personnel data, analyzes changes in representation and pay disparity of women and minorities between 1976 and 1986. Concludes that progress has been made by women and minorities on both fronts, although it has been fairly slow. Also examines equal employment opportunity policies of the Reagan administration and concludes that progress was not thwarted during that period. This conclusion is qualified by the fact that the analysis was done at a point when it may be too early to tell.

169. Mendenhall, Janice. "Roots of the Federal Women's Program." *Civil Service Journal.* 18 (July/September 1977): 21-24.

Discusses the employment status of women Federal employees prior to the establishment of the Federal Women's Program and compares that employment with the types of jobs held by women in the Federal system in 1977. Attributes some of the progress to the work of the Federal Women's Program and Executive Order 11375 which prohibits sex discrimination in Federal employment.

170. Purcell, Deborah Ross. "To FS-2 and Beyond." *Foreign Service Journal.* 62 (July/August 1985): 36-41.

Discusses the lack of advancement into management positions for women at the Agency for International Development (AID). Argues that in the age of shrinking budgets, AID will be forced to make better use of its human resources.

171. Rehfuss, John A. "A Representative Bureaucracy? Women and Minority Executives in California Career Service." *Public Administration Review.* 46 (September/October 1986): 454-460.

Compares senior-level California State executives to their federal Senior Executive Service counterparts. Women and minority executives are then compared to their male non-minority colleagues in California State government.

172. Rytina, Nancy F., and Suzanne M. Bianchi. "Occupational Reclassification and Changes in Distribution by Gender; During the 1970's the Most Important Shift in the Distribution of the Sexes by Occupation Was the Larger Female Representation Among Managers." *Monthly Labor Review.* 107 (March 1984): 11-17.

Examines changes in the occupational distribution of men and women, in the United States focusing on the most dramatic changes--more women moving into managerial positions.

173. U.S. Civil Service Commission. Manpower Statistics Division. *Study of employment of Women in the Federal Government, 1974*, Prepared for the Federal Women's Program. Washington: G.P.O., 1976.

174. U.S. Civil Service Commission. Manpower Statistics Division. *Study of Employment of Women in the Federal Government, 1975.* Washington: G.P.O., 1976.

175. U.S. Office of Personnel Management. Personnel Systems and Oversight Group. *Federal Civilian Work Force Statistics: Affirmative Employment Statistics, 1990.* Washington: G.P.O., 1990. (Published biennially).

Provides statistics for the entire federal work force related to positions of men and women and the grade levels at which they are represented.

176. United States Congress. House. Committee on Foreign Affairs. *Equal Employment Opportunity in the Foreign Affairs Agencies: Hearings, July 29-30, 1987, Before the Subcommittees on International Operations and on Western Hemisphere Affairs.* 100th Cong., 1st sess., 1988.

Deals with minorities and women employed in the field of foreign service. Includes recommendations for improving the recruitment and promotion system currently employed.

177. United States Congress. House. Committee on Foreign Affairs. *The Foreign Service Personnel System at the Department of State: Joint Hearing, October 2, 1990, Before the Subcommittee on International Operations of the Committee on Foreign Affairs, and the Subcommittee on the Civil Service of the Committee on Post Office and Civil Service.* 101st Cong., 2d sess., 1990. S. Hearing 101-87.

Deals with the under-representation of women and minorities at the State Department, including recruitment and promotion issues.

178. U.S. General Accounting Office. *Affirmative Action: National Institutes of Health Does Not Fully Meet Federal Requirements: Report to Congressional Requesters.* Washington: G.A.O., 1986.

Reports that the National Institutes of Health (NIH) has not fully complied with four of eight Equal Employment Opportunity Commission's requirements since its plan was approved in 1983. Argues that this noncompliance may have contributed to the continued under-representation of minorities and women in NIH as of 1984.

179. U.S. General Accounting Office. *Distribution of Male and Female Employees in Four Federal Classification Systems; Report, November 27, 1984.* Washington: G.A.O., 1984.

Presents data on numbers and percents of male and female employees in the General Schedule, the Federal Wage system, the Foreign Service, and the medical professional system at the Veterans Administration's Department of Medicine and Surgery.

180. U.S. General Accounting Office. *EEO at Justice: Progress Made But Under-Representation Remains Widespread; Report to the Chairman.* (Subcommittee on Government Information, Justice and Agriculture, Committee on Government Operations, House of Representatives. Oct. 2, 1990). Washington: G.A.O., 1990.

Reports on the Department of Justice's program to designate six key jobs as the focus of its equal employment opportunity recruiting, hiring, and promotion efforts -- attorney, border patrol agent, correction officer, criminal investigator, deputy U.S. Marshal, and immigration inspector. Justice's data show that representation of minorities and women in its work force has increased over the years. However, under-representation remains widespread. Women are sparsely represented at pay levels above the GS-12 level, and within five of Justice's six key jobs, especially border patrol agent and criminal investigator.

181. U.S. General Accounting Office. *Federal Affirmative Action: Better EEOC Guidance and Agency Analysis of Under-Representation Needed*; Report to the Chairman, Committee on Governmental Affairs, U.S. Senate. Washington, G.A.O., May 10, 1991.

Progress has been made over the last five years in federal agencies but women and minorities are still under-represented-- particularly at higher grade levels. The report finds that the Equal Employment Opportunity Commission (EEOC) has approved agency affirmative action plans even though agencies have not included all the required data or analyses. Further, the report finds that EEOC's approval process has been lengthy and lacks timeliness standards, and federal agencies have not submitted timely affirmative action plans.

182. U.S. General Accounting Office. *State Department: Minorities and Women are Under-Represented in the Foreign Service; Report to the Congress.* Washington: G.A.O., 1989.

183. U.S. General Accounting Office. *Voice of America: Selected Personnel Practices Warrant Management Attention.* Washington: G.A.O., 1989.

Reviews various personnel management practices at Voice of America (VOA) which was prompted by employee allegations about several perennial problems: time and attendance reporting, administration of contracts for purchase order vendors, the grade structure of the foreign language services, the representation of women and minorities, and employment rights of noncitizens.

184. U.S. Office of Personnel Management. *Equal Employment Opportunity Statistics; Federal Civilian Workforce Statistics, 1980.* Washington: O.P.M., 1982

Fifth edition of an annual report which provides statistics on the status of women and minorities in the full-time Federal civilian work force. Results are based on employment statistics within 130 agencies and departments. Covers occupations under Professional, Administrative, Technical, Clerical and Other (PATCO) categories, as well as women and minorities in full-time blue-collar employment within 33 major occupational families.

185. ---. "Women and Public Administration: International Perspectives." *Women & Politics.* 11 (No. 4, 1991): 131 p.

Contents: "Women in Public Administration: A Comparative Perspective." Introduction, by Jane H. Bayes and Jeanne Marie Col; "Women in Public Administration in India," by Hem Lata Swarup and Niroj Sinha; "Women in State Administration in the People's Republic of

Bulgaria," by Nora Ananieva and Evka Razvigorova; "Women in Public Administration in the Netherlands," by Monique Leyenaar; "Women in Public Administration in the Federal Republic of Germany," by Monika Langkau-Herrmann and Ellen Sessar-Karpp; "Women in Public Administration in Finland," by Sirkka Sinkkonen and Eva Hanninen-Salmelin ; "Women in Public Administration in the United States," by Jane H. Bayes; "Women and Public Administration: a Comparative Perspective." Conclusion, by Jane H. Bayes.

186. Yoder, Janice D. "Rethinking Tokenism: Looking Beyond Numbers." *Gender and Society* 5 (June 1991): 178-192.

Refutes Rosabeth Moss Kanter's (1977) work on tokenism, asserting that forced number balancing in the workplace threatens the dominant group (i.e., white males). Argues that tokenism will cause backlash and will, ironically, have the effect of increasing gender discrimination in the forms of sexual harassment, wage inequities, and limited opportunities for promotion.

WOMEN AND RECRUITMENT

187. Slack, James D. "Affirmative Action and City Managers: Attitudes Toward Recruitment of Women." *Public Administration Review*. 47 (March/April 1987): 199-206.

Analyzes support city managers give to the principle of affirmative action. Finds that, by and large, they support affirmative action in principle, but support for mechanisms to implement affirmative action is more tenuous. Concludes that personal characteristics and background of the city manager, as well as presence of an affirmative action plan are major determinants of support for affirmative action.

188. U.S. General Accounting Office. *Achieving Representation of Minorities and Women in the Federal Work Force; Report to the Congress by the Comptroller General of the United States.* Washington: G.A.O., 1980.

Evaluates the efficiency and effectiveness of implementation of section 310 of the Civil Service Reform Act (CSRA) establishing the Minority Recruitment Program; the Federal Equal Employment Opportunity Recruitment Program (FEORP). Specifically, the report evaluates the efficacy of the carrying out CSRA's stated policy of "providing the people of the United States with a competent, honest, and productive Federal work force reflective of the country's diversity." Concludes that implementation was slow to get off the ground, but that agencies basically appeared committed to implementing FEORP.

189. U.S. General Accounting Office. *Administrative Law Judges: Appointment of Women and Social Security Administration Staff Attorneys; Report to the Honorable Sander M. Levin, House of Representatives.* Washington, G.A.O., 1988.

Examines progress being made by federal agencies in appointing women to administrative law judge positions. Also evaluates the Office of Personnel Management's and the Social Security Administration's (SSA) response to congressional direction in 1984 legislation aimed at making SSA staff attorneys more competitive for administrative law judge positions.

190. U.S. Office of Personnel Management. Office of Affirmative Employment Programs. *Annual Report on Implementation of the Federal Equal Opportunity Recruitment Program; Report to Congress.* Washington: G.P.O., 1981.

Outlines Section 310 of the Civil Service Reform Act of 1978 which requires the establishment of the Federal Equal Opportunity Recruitment Program (FEORP). FEORP is "aimed at eliminating the under-representation of minorities in various categories of civil service employment." The report analyzes implementation of FEORP using an "under-representation index," to measure comparisons of women and minority representation in the government with their proportion in the national workforce. Concludes that there were overall gains for minorities and women between November 1978 and May 1980, despite the relatively stable level of employment by the government.

191. U.S. Office of Personnel Management. Office of Affirmative Employment Programs. *Resource Allocation Plan Model for Special Emphasis Program Managers* (Limited Edition). Washington: G.P.O., 1983.

Outlines a Resource Allocation Plan (RAP) model to provide Federal Special Emphasis Program Managers with a process for developing such a plan. It is argued that agencies need a method by which they can identify a reasonable allocation of time and money that will assure a results-oriented program. The RAP is also designed to relate to program managers' participation in the Federal Equal Opportunity Recruitment Program and agency Affirmative Action Plans.

WOMEN AND PROMOTIONS

192. DiPrete, Thomas A., and Whitman T. Soule. "The Organization of Career Lines: Equal Employment Opportunity and Status Advancement in a Federal Bureaucracy." *American Sociological Review*. 51 (June 1986): 295-309.

Examines the consequences of the federal government's efforts during the 1970's to advance upward mobility of lower-level employees. Concludes that these programs helped women and minorities since results show a greater percentage of upper-level, entry-grade positions were filled by promotion after these programs were established.

193. Hale, Mary M. Gender Differences in Career Advancement in the Public Sector. Arizona State University, DPA diss., 1987

Reviews the relationship of gender to equal employment opportunity policy using data from 250 top-level administrators in Arizona State Government, and analyzes differences in career advancement based on gender using a single, integrated model. Differences at the individual level were discovered related to background, formal supports, motivations, career paths, and workplace experience. Within the organizational environment, gender differences were found in the types and sources of support received, workplace experiences, informal networks and mentors, and in commitment to affirmative action. Implications for employment policy are discussed.

194. Lewis, Gregory B. "Equal Employment Opportunity and the Early Career in Federal Employment." *Review of Public Personnel Administration.* 6 (Summer 1986): 1-18.

Study of advancement rates of entry-level employees in the federal civil service during the first eight years of their careers. Results show that white males enter the service in higher grades and more desirable career ladders, and advance further than either women or minorities. And, although race plays a minor part in advancement, gender appears to be an important factor.

195. McEnrue, M.P. "Predicting Attitudes Toward Affirmative Action in Advancement." *Equal Opportunities International (UK).* 7 (No. 1, 1988): 28-31.

Argues that demographic changes, court decisions, and downsizing have caused more emphasis to be placed on affirmative action in advancement rather than selection. Using data from a study of eighty female and minority employees doing low-level administrative and high-level technical or clerical work, the phenomenon of refusing advancement opportunities is examined. Issues such as perceptions that the promotion opportunities are really "phantom," as well as the impact of this phenomenon on attitudes toward affirmative action are explored. Results show that there is a relationship between employees' advancement aspirations, perceptions of opportunity, and their attitudes about affirmative action.

196. South, Scott J., Charles M. Bonjean, William T. Markham, and Judy Corder. "Social Structure and Intergroup Interaction: Men and Women of the Federal Bureaucracy." *American Sociological Review*. 47 (No. 5, 1982): 587-599.

Using survey data from 230 female employees in the federal bureaucracy two theories on the effects of females' proportional representation in work groups on intra- and inter-gender relations are tested. The data support hypotheses of Blau (1977) and Blalock (1967) that suggest that the proportional size of a minority subgroup is negatively related to the frequency of contact with, and amount of social support received from, the majority group. Female proportional representation is also negatively related to the amount of encouragement for promotion employees receive from their male supervisors. Disputes Rosabeth Moss Kanter's (1977) theory that "token" employees face more severe organizational pressures than nontokens. Suggests, however that the dynamics of tokenism described by Kanter tend to offset the negative relationship between female representation and the frequency and quality of male-female associations. Female representation had significant, but counterbalancing, effects on mutual support of female employees.

197. Warner, Rebecca L., and Brent S. Steel. "Affirmative Action in Times of Fiscal Stress and Changing Value Priorities: The Case of Women in Policing." *Public Personnel Management*. 18 (Fall 1989): 291-309.

Examines the probability of women making inroads into non-traditional employment, specifically into municipal police forces. Argues that conservative Political climates as well as recent fiscal trends will thwart affirmative action and make it more difficult for women to get ahead in non-traditional fields and in general.

DISCRIMINATION BASED ON SEX

198. Abramovitz, Mimi. "Blaming Women for Unemployment: Refuting a Myth. *Social Casework*. 65 (November 1984): 547-553.

Discusses and refutes the theory that by seeking employment, women cause the rate of unemployment to rise. Argues that this myth serves to perpetuate the status quo, and identifies reasons for this. Asserts that blaming women for unemployment rates focuses attention away from societal explanations and the real issues of needed change.

199. Castille-Ahrens, Angella. "The Rights of the Pregnant Employee." *Small Business Reports*. 15 (May 1990): 64-67.

Discusses provisions of the Pregnancy Discrimination Act (1978), which makes it unlawful for an employer to discharge, fail to hire, or otherwise discriminate against a women because she is pregnant. Argues that the implementation of this law has been more complex than one might imagine; burgeoning litigation related to maternity leave policies has resulted. As a general rule, the employer is required to reinstate workers who are returning from maternity leaves in the same way other employees would be reinstated after temporary disabilities. Similarly, if indefinite leaves of absence for illness are permitted for some employees, maternity leave cannot be limited. Employers also cannot force a pregnant employee to take a leave of absence if she is capable of performing her job.

200. Crosby, F. "The Denial of Personal Discrimination." *American Behavioral Scientist*. 27 (No. 3): 371-386.

Cites a survey of working women in which results show perceptions that women workers do not receive the rewards they deserve as readily as men. In most cases, however women studied appear to imagine that they personally avoid sex discrimination. Discusses this phenomenon, and outlines the cognitive and emotional barriers to the acknowledgement of personal discrimination. Strategies for dealing with these barriers are given.

201. Dubno, Peter. "Attitudes Toward Women Executives: A Longitudinal Approach." *Academy of Management Journal.* 28 (March 1985): 235-239.

Analyzes attitudes toward women executives in 376 male and 289 female graduate students in 1975, 1978, and 1983. Males consistently had negative attitudes toward females as managers, while their female counterparts were consistently positive. There were no significant differences in attitudes over time. Concludes that women executives will continue to suffer from discrimination and stereotyping by men in the workplace.

202. Faludi, Susan. "Diane Joyce." *Ms.* 16 (January 1988): 62-65, 90-92.

Profiles the first woman road dispatcher in Santa Clara County, California, whose right to her position was affirmed by the Supreme Court in its 1987 Johnson v. Santa Clara County Transportation Agency decision.

203. Green, Lisa Naparstek. "Limitation Periods Under Title VII: Has Time Run Out on the Sovereign Immunity Doctrine?" *Boston University Law Review.* 63 (November 1983): 1157-1185.

"Concludes that the timing requirements for filing suit in federal court under section 717 of title VII are jurisdictional because of the article

III mandates of the sovereign immunity doctrine. Federal courts are therefore summarily barred from hearing cases in which a federal employee has failed to file suit against the government in a timely fashion."

204. Heilman, M.E., and R.F. Martell. "Exposure to Successful Women: Antidote to Sex Discrimination in Applicant Screening Decisions?" *Organizational Behavior and Human Decision Processes.* 37 (1986): 376-390.

Using data from a study of 146 male and female college students, tests whether and under what circumstances exposure to successful women in male-dominated (i.e., non-traditional) occupations eliminates sex bias in selections. Results show that exposure to successful women in these occupations can discourage subsequent discrimination in applicant screening decisions; but, the circumstances under which this is likely to happen are fairly limited. Concludes that an increase in exposure to successful women by itself is not a solution to sex discrimination.

205. Heilman, M.E., M.C. Simon, and D.P. Repper. "Intentionally Favored, Unintentionally Harmed? Impact of Sex-Based Preferential Selection on Self-Perceptions and Self-Evaluation." *Journal of Applied Psychology.* 72 (No. 1, 1987): 62-68.

Using a laboratory setting and male and female undergraduate students, attempts to determine if gender-based differences exist in reactions to preferential selection for leadership positions. Results show that only women's self-perceptions and self-evaluations were negatively affected by the preferential selection method. Gender-based preferential selection led the women studied to devalue their leadership performance, to take less credit for successful outcomes and less interest in continuing in a leadership role. Implications of this research for the implementation of affirmative action programs are discussed. Concludes that how such programs are implemented is vital to their success; merit-based selection processes that selectees are made aware of are recommended.

206. Heilman, M.E., R.F. Martell, and M.C. Simon. "The Vagaries of Sex Bias: Conditions Regulating the Undervaluation, Equivaluation and Overvaluation of Female Job Applicants." *Organizational Behavior and Human Decision Processes*. 41 (1988): 98-110.

Through a study of 241 college students, attempts to determine the circumstances under which women are undervalued, equally valued and overvalued relative to men when they are seeking jobs in male-dominated, non-traditional arenas. Evidence from the study suggests that undervaluation, equal evaluation (equivaluation), and overvaluation of women relative to men exist. Women's ratings only tend to exceed those of men if the job is perceived to be very atypical for a woman to encumber, or unless the woman's performance is verified through information on her abilities.

207. Katz, D. "Sex Discrimination in Hiring: The Influence of Organizational Climate and Need for Approval on Decision Making Behavior." *Psychology of Women Quarterly*. 11 (1987): 11-20.

Using data from a study of male business students, it is argued that organizational climate can either encourage or inhibit discriminatory behavior. Results show that in a "discriminatory climate," female applicants were evaluated less favorably than men in terms of their likelihood of being hired and of fitting in well in the organization. This had no impact on salary decisions, however. Argues that findings suggest that discrimination can be eliminated if organizational cultures which make non-discriminatory decisions are encouraged, or even consciously created. Suggests that certain variables like corporate philosophy, the use of language, and the presence of a significant number of women in management contribute to non-discriminatory environments.

208. Larwood, Laurie, Barbara Gutek, and U. Gattiker. "Perspectives on Institutional Discrimination and Resistance to Change." *Group and Organizational Studies*. 9 (September 1984): 333-352.

Reviews three theories of discrimination--economic, sociological, and psychological, and argues that evidence about efforts to counter discrimination in the workplace demonstrates that little progress has been made. A fourth theory of discrimination named "rational bias" is devised based on managerial behavior made in the context of the organizational culture. It is argued that managers often rely on the perceived preferences of the power structure within and outside their organizations to make decisions. Argues that the higher echelons of organizations must express and demonstrate that discrimination is unacceptable. Concludes that commitment of key, powerful individuals within organizations is essential to eliminating discrimination in the workplace, and argues that, to date, it has typically been lacking.

209. Lewis, Gregory B. "Changing Patterns of Sexual Discrimination in Federal Employment." *Review of Public Personnel Administration*. 7 (No. 2, 1987): 1-8.

Using a sample of Federal personnel records for 1973 and 1982, concludes that the gap between the average grades of white men and women in the General Schedule remains substantial. The gap has, however, narrowed somewhat in recent years as average grades have risen for both men and women. Results suggest that, while women and men are still not rewarded equally for their education and experience, rewards are becoming more equal.

210. Light, Nancy. "Subtle Sexism." *Foreign Service Journal*. 65 (January 1988): 30-35.

Women at the State Department are still grossly underrepresented in upper management's ranks. Asserts that attitudes at State are slow to change, but evidence suggests that younger women are learning to be a source of help and support for each other. Calls for more women to enter the diplomatic service to help achieve and more "critical mass."

211. Peters, Lawrence H., et. al. "Sex Bias and Managerial Evaluations: A Replication and Extension." *Journal of Applied Psychology.* 69 (May 1984): 349-352.

Researches and replicates previous work on sex bias in performance ratings given by supervisors. Concludes that sex bias is not a major factor in determining performance appraisals of employees.

212. Reinhardt, Denise. "Suing the Government for Employment Discrimination." *Journal of Collective Negotiations in the Public Sector.* 20 (No. 2): 167-172.

Outlines processes for filing complaints of discrimination based on factors described in Title VII of the Civil Rights Act of 1964. Reviews the administrative processes Federal, State and local employees must follow, and strongly argues that the process is very convoluted and confusing. Advises anyone considering filing a discrimination complaint against the government to have expert counsel early, else they are likely to be precluded from some parts of the complaint process.

213. Statham, Anne, Eleanor M. Miller, and Hans O. Mauksch, eds. *The Worth of Women's Work: A Qualitative Synthesis.* Albany, NY: State University of New York Press, 1987.

Using data gathered from women in 13 different occupations, examines experiences related to discrimination and oppression. Results show that these women have a remarkable capacity for maintaining their dignity in the face of such treatment.

214. Strauss, Marcy. "Sexist Speech in the Workplace." *Harvard Civil Rights-Civil Liberties Law Review.* 25 (Winter 1990): 1-51.

Argues that the government's interest in eradicating sexist speech from the workplace outweighs, except in some limited circumstances, any First Amendment (i.e., free speech) concerns. Argues that when sexist speech is directed at a "captive audience," or when the speech causes women to be discriminated against in the workplace, the Constitution permits the state to censor it. When the speech is not directed at a particular woman, however, and is not discriminatory, banning sexist speech violates the First Amendment. Concludes with proposals for regulating sexist speech consistent with the Constitutional rights.

215. Watson, Camilla E. "The Pension Game: Age- and Gender-Based Inequities in the Retirement System. *Georgia Law Review.* 25 (Fall 1990): 1-69.

Addresses current issues in both the private retirement and Social Security systems. Outlines and analyzes the effects of pension reform acts such as the Employee Retirement Income Security Act of 1974 (ERISA), the Retirement Equity Act of 1984 (REA); and the Age Discrimination in Employment Act of 1967 (ADEA).

216. U.S. Commission on Civil Rights. *Toward an Understanding of Johnson* (Clearinghouse publication 94). Washington: United States Commission on Civil Rights, 1987.

Analyzes the Supreme Court decision in Johnson v. Santa Clara County Transportation Agency, in which the Court "approved Santa Clara County's decision to promote Diane Joyce, a qualified female applicant, to the position of road dispatcher over Paul Johnson, a better qualified male applicant."

217. Van Fleet, D. D., and J. G. Saurage. "Recent Research on Women in Management." *Akron Business and Economic Review.* 15 (1984): 15-24.

Reviews research and corroborates many previous conclusions about perceptions of discrimination by women, especially in public administration. Concludes that public administration professionals have more negative perceptions of the ability of women to be managers than do those in other disciplines.

218. ---. "Overview: Civil Rights in the 1990s -- Title VII and Employment Discrimination." *Yale Law & Policy Review.* 8 (No. 2, 1990): 197-379.

Partial contents: "The End of the Griggs Economy: Doctrinal Adjustment for the New American Workplace," by Eleanor Holmes Norton; "Court vs. Congress: Judicial Interpretation of the Civil Rights Act and Congressional Response," by Charles Stephen Ralston; "Racial Disparity and Employment Discrimination Law: An Economic Perspective," by James J. Heckman and J. Hoult Verkerke; "The Paradox of Civil Rights," by Richard A. Epstein; "Sexual Harassment as Sex Discrimination: A Defective Paradigm," by Ellen Frankel Paul.

219. ---. "You've Come a Long Way, Baby--But Not As Far As You Thought: While Discrimination is Less Overt, Women Still Aren't Getting to the Top." *Business Week.* October 1, 1984.

Highlights the more subtle issues of discrimination that prevent women from making it to the executive levels.

RESOURCES

Executive Order 11375
AMENDING EXECUTIVE ORDER 11246, RELATING TO EQUAL EMPLOYMENT OPPORTUNITY

It is the policy of the United States Government to provide equal opportunity in Federal employment and in employment by Federal contractors on the basis of merit and without discrimination because of race, color, religion, sex or national origin.

The Congress, by enacting Title VII of the Civil Rights Act of 1964, enunciated a national policy of equal employment opportunity in private employment, without discrimination because of race, color, religion, sex or national origin.

Executive Order No. 11246 of September 24, 1965, carried forward a program of equal employment opportunity in Government employment, employment by Federal contractors and subcontractors and employment under Federally assisted construction contracts regardless of race, creed, color or national origin.

It is desirable that the equal employment opportunity programs provided for in Executive Order No. 11246 expressly embrace discrimination on account of sex.

NOW, THEREFORE, by virtue of the authority vested in me as President of the United States by the Constitution and statutes of the United States, it is ordered that Executive Order No. 11246 of September 24, 1965, be amended as follows:

(1) Section 101 of Part I, concerning nondiscrimination in Government employment, is revised to read as follows:

"SEC. 101. It is the policy of the Government of the United States to provide equal opportunity in Federal employment for all qualified persons, to prohibit discrimination in employment because of race, color, religion, sex, or national origin, and to promote the full realization of equal employment opportunity through a positive, continuing program in each executive department and agency. The policy of equal opportunity applies to every aspect of Federal employment policy and practice."

(2) Section 104 of Part I is revised to read as follows:
"SEC. 104. The Civil Service Commission shall provide for the prompt, fair, and impartial consideration of all complaints of discrimination in Federal employment on the basis of race, color, religion, sex or national origin. Procedures for the consideration of complaints shall include at least one impartial review within the executive department or agency and shall provide for appeal to the Civil Service Commission.....

The amendments to Part I shall be effective 30 days after the date of this order....

Lyndon B. Johnson
The White House, October 13, 1967.

Executive Order 12067
PROVIDING FOR COORDINATION OF
FEDERAL EQUAL EMPLOYMENT OPPORTUNITY PROGRAMS

June 30, 1978

By virtue of the authority vested in me as President of the United States by the Constitution and statutes of the United States, including Section 9 Reorganization Plan Number 1 of 1978 (43 FR 19807), it is ordered as follows:

1-1. *Implementation of Reorganization Plan.*

1-101. The transfer to the Equal Employment Opportunity Commission of all the functions of the Equal Employment Opportunity Coordinating Council, and the termination of that Council, as provided by Section 6 of Reorganization Plan Number 1 of 1978 (43 FR 19807), shall be effective on July 1, 1978.

1-2. *Responsibilities of Equal Employment Opportunity Commission.*

1-201. The Equal Employment Opportunity Commission shall provide leadership and coordination to the efforts of Federal departments and agencies to enforce all Federal statutes, Executive orders, regulations, and policies which require equal employment opportunity without regard to race, color, religion, sex, national origin, age or handicap. It shall strive to maximize effort, promote efficiency, and eliminate conflict, competition, duplication and inconsistency among operations, functions and jurisdictions of the Federal departments and agencies having responsibility for enforcing such statutes, Executive orders, regulations and policies.

1-202. In carrying out its function under this order the Equal Employment Opportunity Commission shall consult with and utilize the special expertise of Federal departments and agencies with equal employment opportunity responsibilities. The Equal Employment

Affirmative Action & Equal Employment Opportunity

Opportunity Commission shall cooperate with such departments and agencies in the discharge of their equal employment responsibilities.

1-203. All Federal departments and agencies shall cooperate with and assist the Equal Employment Opportunity Commission in the performance of its functions under this order and shall furnish the Commission such reports and information as it may request.

1-3. *Specific Responsibilities.*

1-301. To implement its responsibilities under Section 1-2, the Equal Employment Opportunity Commission shall, where feasible:

(a) develop uniform standards, guidelines, and policies defining the nature of employment discrimination on the grounds of race, color, religion, sex, national origin, age or handicap under all Federal statutes, Executive orders, regulations, and policies which require equal employment opportunity;

(b) develop uniform standards and procedures for investigations and compliance reviews to be conducted by Federal departments and agencies under any Federal statute, Executive order, regulation or policy requiring equal employment opportunity;

(c) develop procedures with the affected agencies, including the use of memoranda of understanding, to minimize duplicative investigations or compliance reviews of particular employers or classes of employers or others covered by Federal statute, Executive order, regulation or policy requiring equal employment opportunity;

(d) ensure that Federal departments and agencies develop their own standards and procedures for undertaking enforcement actions when compliance with equal employment opportunity requirements of any Federal statute, Executive order, regulation or policy cannot be secured by voluntary means;

(e) develop uniform record-keeping and reporting requirements concerning employment practices to be utilized by all Federal departments and agencies having equal employment enforcement responsibilities;

(f) provide for the sharing of compliance records, findings, and supporting documentation among Federal departments and agencies responsible for ensuring equal employment opportunity;

(g) develop uniform training programs for the staff of Federal departments and agencies with equal employment opportunity responsibilities;

(h) assist all Federal departments and agencies with equal employment opportunity responsibilities in developing programs to provide appropriate publications and other information for those covered and those protected by Federal equal employment opportunity statutes, Executive orders, regulations, and policies; and

(i) initiate cooperative programs, including the development of memoranda of understanding between agencies, designed to improve the coordination of equal employment opportunity compliance and enforcement.

1-302. The Equal Employment Opportunity Commission shall assist the Civil Service Commission, or its successor, in establishing uniform job-related qualifications and requirements for job classifications and descriptions for Federal employees involved in enforcing all Federal equal employment opportunity provisions.

1-303. The Equal Employment Opportunity Commission shall issue such rules, regulations, policies, procedures or orders as it deems necessary to carry out its responsibilities under this order...

Jimmy Carter

The White House
June 29, 1978.

TIME LIMITS FOR INITIATING THE EEO PROCESS UNDER 29 C.F.R. PART 1614

A) An individual complainant or his/her representative must contact an EEO counselor within *45 days* of the incident causing concern, or of the effective date of the personnel action(s), or the date that the complainant became aware of the act or action.

B) Class complainants or their representatives must contact an EEO counselor within *45 days* of the incident causing concern, or of the effective date of the personnel action(s).

Note: The Director, EEOC may extend these time limits under certain conditions.

Pre-Complainant Counseling
Upon being contacted by the aggrieved employee(s) or their representative, the EEO counselor will issue a notice of final counseling within *30 days*. During this period the counselor makes inquiries and attempts to informally resolve the matter.

If the informal resolution cannot be accomplished in the respective in the allotted period, the Counselor must provide the complainant(s) with a notice of their right to file a formal EEO complaint. The complainant has *15 days* from receipt of this notice to file a formal complaint.

Filing the Formal EEO Complaint
An aggrieved employee or applicant must file a formal complaint in writing within *15 days* after either the:

1. Initial Notice of Right to File a Formal Complaint; or
2. Notice of Final Interview with EEO Counselor.

The formal complaint must be signed and be based only on those issues for which the complainant(s) received EEO counseling.

Exception: Exceptions to filing an EEO complaint without counseling are limited to charges of restraining, interference, coercion, discrimination or reprisal in connection with presentation or processing a complaint. Under these conditions, an aggrieved employee may file a formal complaint within 15 calendar days of the alleged occurrence.

Agency Acceptance of Complaint

Upon receipt of the Formal Complaint, the Director, EEO, will notify the complainant of the agency's acceptance or rejection of the complaint in whole or in part. Those complaints or parts thereof which are accepted by the agency are assigned to an EEO Investigator to develop a report of the facts surrounding the complaint. The agency has *180 days* from the date the complaint was filed to complete the investigation.

Decisions and Appeals

A copy of the investigation file is provided to the complainant; within *30 days* of receipt the complainant may request and EEOC hearing or a final decision from the agency. If the complainant does not respond or requests an immediate final decision, the agency will issue a decision based on a review of the investigation file within *90 days*. If an EEOC hearing is requested by the complainant an administrative judge will rule and order a remedy (if discrimination is discovered) within *180 days* of the request for a hearing.

Within *60 days* of receipt of the administrative judge's notification, the agency must issue its final decision. The agency may reject or modify the findings and conclusions or the relief ordered by the judge. If no action is taken, the judge's decision becomes final.

Once the complainant receives the agency's final decision, he or she may appeal it to the EEOC within *30 days*, or file a civil action in a U.S. District Court within *90 days*.

CHAPTER 4

Sexual Harassment

"Those in power want only to perpetuate it." Justice William O. Douglas.

THE ISSUES & THE PREVENTION

220. Arriola, Elvia R. "'What's The Big Deal?' Women in the New York City Construction Industry and Sexual Harassment Law, 1970-1985." *Columbia Human Rights Law Review.* 22 (Fall 1990): 21-71.

Argues sexual harassment law was the product of political outcry and mobilization of a predominantly white, middle-class women's movement. As a result, the law had a greater impact on changing masculine sexual attitudes and behavior in middle-class, white-collar work settings. Further argues that sexual harassment laws did not address the "different" problems that women who work in non-traditional, blue-collar fields face.

221. Barnett, Edith. "Sexual Harassment: A Continuing Source of Litigation in the Workplace." *Trial.* 25 (June 1989): 34-38.

Discusses changes to sexual harassment law based on recent Guidance promulgated by the Equal Employment Opportunity Commission in recent court decisions. Argues that three areas have been "left open" by the Supreme Court's 1986 Vinson decision. These include definitions of "welcomeness" of sexual conduct alleged to constitute sexual harassment, types of sexual conduct actionable as sexual harassment under Title VII, and standards for holding employers liable for sexual harassment in the workplace.

222. Bennett-Alexander, Dawn D. "Hostile Environment Sexual Harassment: A Clearer View." *Labor Law Journal.* 42 (March 1991): 131-143.

Attempts to clarify "hostile environment" sexual harassment, and the kinds of evidence which may be presented to show that the actions of an alleged offender are welcome or unwelcome. Implications for liability to employers under hostile environment sexual harassment are discussed.

223. Brophy, Beth. "Sexual Dilemmas of the Modern Office." *U.S. News & World Report.* 101 (December 8, 1986): 55-58.

Outlines problems that arise from office romances and how they are handled in the workplace. Surmises that oftentimes, one person leaves the organization voluntarily or by request. Includes a sidebar on sexual harassment.

224. Cates, Jo. "Sexual Harassment: What Every Woman and Man Should Know." *Library Journal.* 110 (July 1985): 23-29.

Provides guidelines for employees about what sexual harassment is, the laws that protect them, the laws that do not protect them, and the steps that can be taken to fight sexual harassment in the workplace.

225. Clark, Charles S. "Sexual Harassment." *CQ Researcher.* 1 (August 9, 1991): 537-560.

Discusses the broadening of the legal definition of sexual harassment. Delineates new inclusions under the rubric of sexual harassment including lascivious comments, off-color jokes and "leering." Claims that these gray areas raise debates over First Amendment rights. Argues that since employers are being held responsible for sexual harassment in the workplace, many organizations have adopted guidelines and grievance procedures, yet the courts are still crowded with sexual harassment complaints.

226. Cohen, Lynn Renee. "Nonverbal (Mis)Communication Between Managerial Men and Women." *Business Horizons.* 26 (January/February 1983): 13-17.

Surveys the effects of communication patterns called courting cues and quasi-courting cues. Believes that "by changing or minimizing certain characteristic patterns of nonverbal communication, women can gain better control over difficult situations at work and reduce the level of sexual harassment."

227. David, Marilyn H. "A Title VII Cause of Action for the Sexually Harassed Federal Employee?" *Air Force Law Review.* 23 (1982-1983): 254-270.

Concludes that there has been no legal or procedural definition of section 717 of Title VII to date. No clear-cut guidance has been established related to the breadth of section 717 vis-a-vis sexual harassment in federal employment. Argues that "determinative weight" must be given to Congress' goal to eradicate such discrimination in the federal sector just as it has been in the private sector.

228. Ehrenreich, Nancy S. "Pluralist Myths and Powerless Men: The Ideology of Reasonableness in Sexual Harassment Law. *Yale Law Journal.* 99 (April 1990): 1177-1234.

Examines the role of the "reasonableness" standard in "hostile work environment" sexual harassment cases under Title VII. Offers an explanation for how the reasonable person test can remain legitimate even though there are analytical weaknesses. Questions the use of a standard that favors the status quo being used to identify discriminatory practices.

229. Ely, John Hart. "On Living Lies for Professional Reasons." *Constitutional Commentary.* 9 (Winter 1992): 1-4.

Comments on the Thomas confirmation hearings, the question of perjury and of women and men in the workplace.

230. Estrich, Susan. "Sex At Work. *Stanford Law Review.* 43 (April 1991): 813-861.

Examines the development of workplace sexual harassment law as an application of Title VII of the Civil Rights Act of 1964.

231. Federally Employed Women. *Combating Sexual Harassment: A Federal Worker's Guide.* Washington: Federally Employed Women, Inc., 1991.

A handbook on sexual harassment which dispels several myths about what harassment is and who gets harassed. Outlines the legal and historical definitions of sexual harassment and gives steps for preventing and combating sexual harassment in formal as well as informal ways.

232. Fritz, Norma R. "Sexual Harassment and the Working Woman." *Personnel.* 66 (February 1989): 4.

Analyzes results from a 1988 *Working Woman* survey on attitudes about sexual harassment. Results show that sexual harassment is widespread, and that complaint rates are highest in companies where women make up a smaller percentage of the workforce. Argues that the best prevention of sexual harassment will come from formal, serious policies and complaint processes.

233. Gibbs, Nancy. "Office Crimes: In a Matter of Hours, A New Vocabulary of Laws and Risks and Expectations Entered the Language of the Factory Floor and the Tower Suite." *Time.* 138 (October 21, 1991): 52-64.

Discusses the rapid pace with which organizations have had to learn to understand and deal with the issue of sexual harassment. Analyzes some of the factors contributing to this revelation in the American workplace. Defines sexual harassment as, "... an abuse of power in which a worker who depends for her livelihood and professional survival on the good will of a superior is made to feel vulnerable."

234. Gutek, Barbara A. *Sex in the Workplace.* San Francisco, CA: Jossey-Bass, 1985.

Outlines issues related to sexual harassment in the workplace, and defines practices that constitute sexual harassment. Describes the negative effects of sexual harassment on women, and successful strategies for combating it.

235. Hauck, Vern E., and Thomas G. Pearce. "Vinson: Sexual Harassment and Employer Response." *Labor Law Journal.* 38 (December 1987): 770-775.

Discusses the Supreme Court's 1986 decision in *Meritor Savings Bank vs. Vinson* in which the plaintiff won a suit on the basis of Title VII sexual harassment. Concludes that the practical implications of Vinson for employers is that they must develop, adopt, implement, and enforce policies prohibiting sexual harassment. Argues that employers who have no formal policy cannot demonstrate a "good faith" effort to eliminate sexual harassment in their organizations.

236. Kandel, William L. "Sexual Harassment: Persistent, Prevalent, but Preventable." *Employee Relations Law Journal*. 14 (Winter 1988/1989): 439-451.

Argues that there is a need to convince employers and employees of their personal interest in eradicating sexual harassment. Discusses a recent survey of federal employees that indicates that sexual harassment continues, relatively unchanged. Discusses prevention as the best solution for abating sexual harassment in the workplace. Elements of such a program of prevention would include a clearly written policy coupled with a well-defined process for hearing and investigating complaints. Also argues that since the 1986 *Vinson* decision, it is important to inform employees that sexual harassment can result in liability for related offenses.

237. Kantrowitz, Barbara. "Striking a Nerve." *Newsweek*. 118 (October 21, 1991): 34-40.

Comments on the effect the Congressional testimony of Anita Hill had. Argues that millions of American women saw and heard themselves through Anita Hill, and that event will spark an incredible burgeoning of sexual harassment claims. Also argues that women are fed up with the fact that men simply do not understand what sexual harassment is all about.

238. Kaufman, Leslie. "Sexual Harassment." *Government Executive*. 74 (April 1992): 42-45.

Examines various personnel practices in Federal agencies in response to the growing awareness of sexual harassment in the workplace. Explores various new training programs the government is implementing, and outlines the streamlined complaint procedures that are being developed.

239. Linenberger, Patricia. "What Behavior Constitutes Sexual Harassment?" *Labor Law Journal*. 34 (April 1983): 238-247.

Outlines and analyzes Equal Employment Opportunity Commission Guidelines, several governmental agency definitions, as well as two research projects to identify less "blatant" types of sexual harassment. Presents ten factors which should be considered by employers and employees when evaluating behavior for potential sexual harassment liability.

240. Meier, Sara Beth. "Expanding Title VII to Prohibit a Sexually Harassing Work Environment." *Georgetown Law Journal*. 70 (October 1981): 345-364.

Examines the United States Court of Appeals for the District of Columbia Circuit's decision in *Bundy v. Jackson*. Bundy, a vocational rehabilitation specialist at the District of Columbia Department of Corrections, sued her employer under Title VII claiming that, by allowing her supervisors to make repeated sexual advances, her employer subjected her to sexual discrimination. The court ruled that a work environment in which an employer condones sexual harassment is sufficient to constitute a discriminatory "condition of employment."

241. Morehead, Joe. "Federal Policies and Publications on Sexual Harassment." *Technical Services Quarterly*. 3 (Spring-Summer 1986): 253-266.

Examines federal policies and publications on sexual harassment by reviewing documentation published by the federal establishment.

242. Morlacci, Maria. "Sexual Harassment Law and the Impact of Vinson." *Employee Relations Law Journal*. 13 (Winter 1987-88): 501-519.

Comments on the Supreme Court's 1986 ruling in *Meritor Savings Bank v. Vinson*, and argues that the decision confirms the Court's acknowledgement of the detrimental effects of "hostile environment" sexual harassment. Concludes that the Vinson decision represents an improvement for sexual harassment law in that it gives further protection to victims of sexual harassment.

243. Murray, P.J. "Employment: Beware of "Hostile Environment" Sexual Harassment." *Duquesne Law Review*. 26 (Winter 1988): 461-484.

Focuses on hostile environment sexual harassment. Broken into three parts covering standards for assessing "hostile environment" behavior, responsibilities of employers and employees in claims of hostile environment sexual harassment, and recommendations for employers who are trying to eradicate harassment in the workplace.

244. ---. "Participation of Women: The Reality in 1985." *Forum (Council of Europe)* January, 1985. (whole issue).

Partial contents: "Women and Political Power in Europe," by M. Sineau; "Running the Country? -- The Role of Rural Women," by A. Mangrioti; "Sexual Violence and the Law in Italy," by G. Modona; "Sex

Discrimination in the United Kingdom," by D. Pannick; "Unions and the Working Woman," by H. Horburger; "Resolving Sexual Harassment in Canada, by S. M'Gonigle; "A Woman's Life in Switzerland," by G. Nanchen; "Violence Against Women: A Scandinavian Perspective," by A. Snare.

245. Powell, Gary N. "Sexual Harassment: Confronting the Issue of Definition." *Business Horizons*. 26 (July-August 1983): 24-28.

Compares the Equal Employment Opportunity Commission's and the Office of Personnel Management's definitions of sexual harassment to results of a survey of 101 full-time working women in a medium-sized New England city. Concludes that when organizations develop their own definitions, as recommended, and apply them objectively and consistently, they free management from liability and employees from sexual harassment.

246. Robinson, Robert K., Delaney J. Kirk, and James D. Powell. "Sexual Harassment: New Approaches for a Changed Environment." *SAM Advanced Management Journal*. 52 (Autumn 1987): 15-18, 47.

Discusses the Supreme Court's ruling in *Meritor Savings Bank v. Vinson* and the ways in which that decision broadened the definition of sexual harassment by making it management's responsibility to prevent it. Argues that organizations would be well served to establish, review, and evaluate policies on sexual harassment in order to avoid costly law suits.

247. Ross, Cynthia S., and Robert E. England. "State Governments' Sexual Harassment Policy Initiatives." *Public Administration Review*. 47 (May-June 1987): 259-262.

Studies state government initiatives to deal with sexual harassment in the workplace. Finds that most states have taken positive steps to address sexual harassment through statewide policies, agency/departmental policies, and training programs in sexual harassment.

248. Smith, Kathleen A. "Employer Liability for Sexual Harassment: Inconsistency Under Title VII." *Catholic University Law Review.* 37 (Fall 1987): 245-277.

Argues that the 1986 *Meritor Savings Bank v. Vinson* decision may cause employers to ignore a situation when they suspect that an employee, who has not come forward and directly informed the employer, is being sexually harassed.

249. Spann, Jeri. "Dealing Effectively with Sexual Harassment: Some Practical Lessons from One City's Experience." *Public Personnel Management.* 19 (Spring 1990): 53-68.

Outlines the issues of gender versus sexual harassment, and delineates a "hierarchy of problem behaviors and effects," in the context of the City of Madison, Wisconsin's experience with sexual harassment between 1979 and 1985. Also analyzes the major findings of the Supreme Court's decision in *Meritor Savings Bank, FSB v. Vinson, et. al.*, and the effects and implications of that decision on public administration. Recommendations for future action are given.

250. Stringer, Donna M., Helen Remick, Jan Salibury, and Angela Ginorio. "The Power Behind Sexual Harassment: An Employer's Guide to Solutions." *Public Personnel Management.* 19 (Spring 1990): 43-52.

Discusses and applies three models of power--achieved (that which someone earns), ascribed (that which someone is given), and situational (that which someone has as a result of a situation)--to sexual harassment. Argues that management solutions must be derived from an understanding of individual cases and the power model, sexual relationship, and motivation at play. Discusses seven reasons and motivations for sexual harassment and offers appropriate management responses for each.

251. Terpstra, David E. "Who Gets Sexually Harassed?" *Personnel Administrator*. 34 (March 1989): 84-86.

Analyzes characteristics of women who file sexual harassment charges by age, education level, and occupation, as well as the outcomes of the sexual harassment cases. Recommends creating formal sexual harassment policies that describe, in clear terms, unacceptable behavior and the penalties that will be associated with engaging in certain behavior.

252. U.S. Bureau of Mines. *Training in the Prevention of Sexual Harassment*. Washington: U.S. Bureau of Mines, 1987.

Handbook of recommendations and actions related to several facets of sexual harassment. Includes sex role stereotyping (SRS); defining sex discrimination (DSD); defining sexual harassment (DSH); identifying and dealing with sexual harassment (IDD); personal responsibility for prevention (PRP); and actions steps (ACT).

253. U.S. Commission on Civil Rights. *Sex Harassment on the Job: A Guide for Employers*. Washington: United States Commission on Civil Rights, Massachusetts Advisory Committee, 1983.

Contents: Sexual Harassment -- Some Basic Questions; Sexual Harassment and the Law; Actions You Can Take in Your Organization; Model Questionnaire on Sexual Harassment; Sample Policy on Sexual Harassment; Bibliography on Sexual Harassment; Equal Employment Opportunity Commission's Guidelines on Sexual Harassment.

254. United States Congress. House. Committee on Post Office and Civil Service. Subcommittee on Investigations. *Sexual harassment in the Federal Government.* 96th Cong., 2d sess., 1980. No. 96-11.

255. U.S. Merit Systems Protection Board. *Sexual Harassment in the Federal Workplace: Is It a Problem?* Washington: G.P.O., 1981.

Outlines and examines federal workers' views on sexual harassment in the workplace, and perceptions on the extent of sexual harassment that exists in the federal workplace. Discusses characteristics of victims and perpetrators of sexual harassment. Describes incidence of sexual harassment, and its impact on cost. Outlines the available remedies and their effectiveness, and reports general findings, conclusions, and policy and practical recommendations for the future.

256. U.S. Merit Systems Protection Board. *Sexual Harassment in the Federal Government: An Update.* Washington: MSPB, 1988.

Reports on the nature and frequency of sexual harassment in the federal workplace. Concludes that sexual harassment remains widespread. Forty-two percent of all women respondents to the survey reported experiencing some form of uninvited sexual attention. Reports that the most likely victims of sexual harassment are women between the ages of 20 and 44, who are single or divorced, have some college education, work in nontraditional jobs, or work in predominately male environments. Includes discussion of what employees and management have done to combat sexual harassment in the workplace, and makes recommendations for future action.

257. U.S. Office of Personnel Management, Supervisory and Communications Training Center. *Workshop on Sexual Harassment.* Washington: G.P.O., 1980.

Two volume set which includes a trainer's manual and a participant's manual. Attempts to introduce participants to the nature and seriousness of the problem of sexual harassment in the Federal workforce. Emphasizes and teaches awareness to the problem as the most important means of preventing sexual harassment. Both general and specific instruction is given.

258. Wilds, Nancy G. "Sexual Harassment in the Military." *HINERVA: Quarterly Report on Women and the Military.* 8 (Winter 1990): 1-16.

Discusses efforts at the Department of Defense (DoD) to quell sex discrimination and sexual harassment. Unfortunately, despite efforts at high levels in DoD to eliminate gender discrimination on the job, sexual harassment continues to be a serious problem in all branches of the Armed Services.

259. ---. "Sexual Harassment Claims of Abusive Work Environment Under Title VII. *Harvard Law Review.* 97 (April 1984): 1449-1467.

Examines differences between "disparate treatment" sexual harassment, and sexual harassment based on a theory that "pervasive workplace harassment may constitute discrimination by creating an 'abusive working environment.'" Argues that differences between these two issues will make innovative judicial approaches imperative when dealing with abusive environment claims.

RELEVANT LAWS AND REGULATIONS

Chronology of Sexual Harassment Legal Mandates

(From EEO Counselor's Training Manual--U.S. Office of Personnel Management.)

The Civil Rights Act of 1964 - Title VII of the Civil Rights Act of 1964 prohibits discrimination in employment based on sex. Harassment on the basis of sex is a violation of Section 703 of Title VII. The courts have generally ruled that employees do have Title VII claim when a job is lost because of refusal to submit to sexual advances, or, when an offensive work environment is created as a result of sexually harassing behavior.

Williams v. Saxbe 1976 - The first ruling to support a female complainant in a sexual harassment case. The Federal District Court held that the supervisor created an artificial barrier to employment that was placed before one gender (females) and not another (males). It reasoned that if the supervisor's policy was to base employment conditions on sexual submission, then it also was the employer's policy. Since the supervisor was found to have made similar advances to other female subordinates, then a discriminatory condition of employment was established.

Barnes v. Costel 1977 - Sexual harassment is prohibited in Federal employment and is covered by the sex discrimination provision of the Equal Employment Opportunity Act of 1972 and redressable throughout the discrimination complaint procedure. A single instance of sexual harassment may form the basis of an EEO complaint or civil suit.

Miller v. Bank of America 1979 - The employer is still responsible for sexual harassment behavior of its supervisors even if the employer has an established policy against sexual harassment. This is critical for all managers to know; the establishment of a policy is not enough. They must do more.

Williams v. Civiletti 1980 - Unwelcome sexual advances as a term and condition of employment can constitute sexual harassment even if at one time the advances were encouraged and/or returned.

EEO Guidelines 1980 - EEOC incorporated sexual harassment into the "Guidelines on Discrimination Because of Sex," making sexual harassment a prohibited practice. Section 1604.11 of the EEOC's Guidelines defines sexual harassment as: the deliberate or repeated unsolicited verbal comments, gestures, or physical contact of a sexual nature that are unwelcome. Within the Federal Government, a supervisor who uses implicit or explicit coercive sexual behavior to control, influence or affect the career, salary, or job of an employee is engaging in sexual harassment. Similarly, an employee or an agency business is engaging in sexual harassment. Finally, any employee who participates in deliberate or repeated unsolicited verbal comments, gestures, or, physical contact of a sexual nature that is unwelcome and interferes in work productivity is also engaging in sexual harassment.

EEOC's Guidelines also state that prevention is the best tool for elimination of sexual harassment: "An employer should take all steps necessary to prevent sexual harassment from occurring, such as affirmatively aiding the subject, expressing strong approval, developing appropriate sanctions, informing employees of their right to raise, and how to raise, the issue of sexual harassment under Title VII, and developing methods to sensitize all concerned."

Bundy v. Jackson (U.S. Court of Appeals for D.C.) - The significant ruling in this case was that sexual harassment, in and of itself, is a violation of the law and further proof is not required that the employee was penalized or lost specific job benefits.

EEOC v. Sage Realty 1981 - Requiring employees to wear sexually provocative clothing as a condition of employment is a violation of Title VII and Guidelines.

Wright v. Methodist Youth Services 1981 - Unwelcome sexual advances are prohibited under Title VII even when the parties involved are of the same sex.

Katz v. Dole 1983 - The employer is responsible for the acts of sexual harassment on the part of supervisors or co-workers. The employer is liable when it fails to respond to acts of sexual harassment. Merely indicating the existence of an official policy against such harassment does not constitute an adequate response.

Banett v. Omaha Bank 1984 - The employer is not liable for acts of sexual harassment between co-workers when the employer responds promptly to the complaint of sexual harassment (conducts a full investigation, directs that the harassing behavior end, and indicates the disciplinary consequences should the conduct continue).

Meritor Savings Bank v. Vinson 1986 - The employer is responsible for acts of sexual harassment by its supervisors even when the company has not been informed of the conduct. To prove discrimination under Title VII, the victim need not show that the conduct had a tangible income impact but that it created a "hostile environment."

Robinson v. Jacksonville Shipyards 1991 - The employer is responsible for investigating and eradicating all forms of sexual harassment or sex discrimination or retaliation. Further, the employer must issue a sexual harassment policy, a statement of prohibited conduct, a schedule of penalties for misconduct, and procedures through which employees can lodge complaints.

Ellison v. Brady 1991 - A female plaintiff has a legitimate hostile environment sexual harassment case when she alleges conduct which a "reasonable woman considers sufficiently severe or pervasive to alter conditions of employment and create an abusive working environment."

29 Code of Federal Regulations, Chapter XIV, Part 1604
GUIDELINES ON DISCRIMINATION BECAUSE OF SEX

Section 1604.11 Sexual harassment.

a) Harassment on the basis of sex is a violation of Sec. 703 of Title VII. Unwelcome sexual advances, requests for sexual favors, and other verbal or physical conduct of a sexual nature constitute sexual harassment when (1) submission to such conduct is made either explicitly or implicitly a term or condition of an individual's employment, (2) submission to or rejection of such conduct by an individual is used as the basis for employment decisions affecting such individual, or (3) such conduct has the purpose or effect of unreasonably interfering with an individual's work performance or creating an intimidating, hostile, or offensive working environment.

b) In determining whether alleged conduct constitutes sexual harassment, the Commission will look at the record as a whole and at the totality of the circumstances, such as the nature of the sexual advances and the context in which the alleged incidents occurred. The determination of the legality of a particular action will be made from the facts, on a case by case basis.

c) Applying general Title VII principles, an employer, employment agency, joint apprenticeship committee or labor organization (hereinafter collectively referred to as "employer") is responsible for its acts and those of its agents and supervisory employees with respect to sexual harassment regardless of whether the specific acts complained of were authorized or even forbidden by the employer and regardless of whether the employer knew or should have known of their occurrence. The Commission will examine the circumstances of the particular employment relationship and the job functions performed by the individual in determining whether an individual acts in either a supervisory or agency capacity.

d) With respect to conduct between fellow employees, an employer is responsible for acts of sexual harassment in the work place where the employer (its agents or supervisory employees) knows or should have known of the conduct, unless it can show that it took immediate and appropriate corrective action.

e) An employer may also be responsible for the acts of non-employees, with respect to sexual harassment of employees in the work place, where the employer (its agents or supervisory employees) knows or should have known of the conduct and fails to take immediate and appropriate corrective action. In reviewing these cases the Commission will consider the extent of the employer's control and other legal responsibility which the employer may have with respect to the conduct of such non-employees.

f) Prevention is the best tool for the elimination of sexual harassment. An employer should take all steps necessary to prevent sexual harassment from occurring, such as affirmatively raising the subject, expressing strong disapproval, developing appropriate sanctions, informing employees of their right to raise and how to raise the issue of harassment under Title VII, and developing methods to sensitize all concerned.

g) Other related practices: Where employment opportunities or benefits are granted because of an individual's submission to the employer's sexual advances or requests for sexual favors, the employer may be held liable for unlawful sex discrimination against other persons who were qualified for but denied that employment or benefit.

RESOURCES

Organizations Offering Assistance to Victims of Sexual Harassment

1) American Bar Association, 1800 M Street, NW., Suite 200 South Lobby, Washington, DC 20036, (202) 331-2200.

2) American Civil Liberties Union (Women's Rights Project), 132 West 43rd Street, New York, NY 10036, (212) 944-9800.

3) DC Bar--Office of Public Lawyer Referral and Information Service, 1426 H Street, NW., Washington, DC 20005, (202) 331-4365.

4) DC Office of Human Rights, 2000 14th Street, NW., 3rd Floor, Washington, DC 20009, (202) 939-8740.

5) Equal Employment Opportunity Commission, 2401 E Street, NW., Washington, DC 20415, (202) 634-6700.

6) Federally Employed Women Legal and Education Fund, P.O. Box 4830, Washington, DC 20008, (202) 462-5235.

7) Institute of Public Representation--Georgetown University Law Center, 600 New Jersey Avenue, NW., Washington, DC 20001, (202) 624-8390.

8) Lawyer's Committee for Civil Rights Under the Law, 1400 I Street, NW., Washington, DC 20005, (202) 321-1212.

9) NOW--Legal Defense Fund, Attn: Intake Department, 99 Hudson Street, Suite 1201, New York, NY 10013, (202) 925-6635.

10) National Women's Law Center, 1616 P Street, NW., Suite 100, Washington, DC 20036, (202) 328-5160.

11) U.S. Office of Personnel Management, 1900 E Street, NW., Washington, DC 20415, (202) 606-1212.

12) Trial Lawyers for Public Justice, 1625 Massachusetts Avenue, NW., Suite 100, Washington, DC 20036, (202) 638-3143.

13) Wider Opportunities for Women (WOW), 1325 G street, NW., Lower Level, Washington, DC 20005, (202) 638-3143.

14) Women's Action for Good Employment Standards (WAGES), c/o Institute for Research on Women's Health, 1616 18th Street, NW., #109B, Washington, DC 20009, (202) 483-8643.

15) Women Employed Institute, 22 West Monroe Street, Suite 1400, Chicago, IL 60603, (312) 782-3902.

16) Women's Law Project, 125 South 9th Street, Suite 401, Philadelphia, PA 19107, (215) 928-9801.

17) Women's Legal Defense Fund, 1875 Connecticut Avenue, NW., Suite 710, Washington, DC 20009, (202) 986-2600.

18) Women Students' Sexual Harassment Caucus, Department of Applied Psychology, Ontario Institute for Studies in Education, 252 Bloor Street West, Toronto, Ontario M5S 1V6.

CHAPTER 5

Pay Equity

"Money doesn't talk, it swears." Bob Dylan.

THE RESEARCH & THE DEBATE

260. Bellak, Alvin O., Marsh W. Bates, and Daniel M. Glasner. "Job Evaluation: Its Role in the Comparable Worth Debate." *Public Personnel Management.* 12 (Winter 1983): 418-424.

Examines research by D. J. Treiman (1979) in a National Academy of Sciences project and Treiman and H. I. Hartmann's (1981) report on women, work, and wages. Concludes that job evaluation systems cannot gain wide acceptance and validity to the extent that is necessary to lend support to implementation of comparable worth. Argues that education about and adherence to equal employment opportunity laws are the most appropriate and surest ways to achieve pay equity.

261. Bergmann, Barbara R. "Does the Market for Women's Labor Need Fixing?" *Journal of Economic Perspectives.* 3 (Winter 1989): 43-60.

Argues that wage disparities between men and women can be attributed to set-asides of jobs for men and women, as well as history and traditional attitudes about employment based on gender. Analyzes affirmative action programs as well as job evaluation systems that serve to mitigate pay inequities, and concludes that the government needs to take action by issuing guidelines to pressure organizations to raise wages for female-dominated occupations.

262. Blau, Francine D., and Andrea H. Beller. "Trends in Earnings Differentials by Gender, 1971-1981." *Industrial and Labor Relations Review.* 41 (July 1988): 513-529.

Using a non-traditional method of measuring gender differences in pay (i.e., number of hours and weeks worked), asserts that strides were made in the 1970's toward a more equal male-female earnings ratio. Also demonstrates that, although the effect was not very great, there was a decline in women's relative return on education and entrance into male-dominated careers.

263. Booker, Sharon, and Camille L. Nuckolls. "Legal and Economic Aspects of Comparable Worth." *Public Personnel Management.* 15 (Summer 1986): 189-206.

An analysis of legislative history and current case law shows that women were also influenced not to participate in the labor market by certain federal governmental programs and policies that promoted conformity to the traditional sex roles. Suggests several measures for implementing comparable worth such as reducing evaluator bias by evaluating all jobs within an organization; not relying on marketplace value data, which has traditionally discriminated against women; and using a single job evaluation system within organizations since different evaluation systems tend to devalue positions typically encumbered by women and minorities.

264. Borjas, G.J. "The Measurement of Race and Gender Wage Differentials: Evidence from the Public Sector." *Industrial and Labor Relations.* 37 (October 1983): 97-110.

Using a sample of federal employees from the Central Personnel Data File, examines pay disparities based on race and gender. Results show that federal agencies which have larger pay differences based on race are also more likely to have pay differences based on gender. Results also show that pay disparity for black women is more closely related to gender than race. Concludes that there is a strong relationship between pay disparities based on gender and pay disparities based on race. This, it is argued, is evidence that the same factors are responsible for wage discrimination in these cases.

265. Chi, Keon S. "Comparable Worth in State Governments." *State Government.* 27 (November 1984): 4-6.

Discusses that state of comparable worth legislation in State governments. Outlines programs in four states--Minnesota, New Mexico, Iowa and Washington--where implementation of compensation plans to reduce pay disparities between men and women has already begun.

266. Chi, Keon S. "Comparable Worth in State Government: Trends and Issues. *Policy Studies Review.* 5 (May 1986): 800-814.

Provides an overview of state comparable worth policies and activities, focusing on longitudinal trends and issues. Presents preliminary findings of three surveys conducted for The Council of State Governments.

267. Evans, Sara M., and Barbara J. Nelson. "Initiating a Comparable Worth Wage Policy in Minnesota: Notes from the Field." *Policy Studies Review.* 5 (May 1986): 849-862.

Analyzes Minnesota State's pay equity policy from a "field" perspective half way through the inception and implementation of the program. Provides a detailed chronology of the initiation of the State's pay equity policy, and appraises the Minnesota experience vis-a-vis national efforts to adopt and implement pay equity policies.

268. Flammang, Janet A. "Effective Implementation: The Case of Comparable Worth in San Jose." *Policy Studies Review*. 5 (May 1986): 815-837.

   Argues that the implementation of comparable worth adjustments given to some employees by the city of San Jose, California, in 1981 was effective. Examines possible reasons for this achievement.

269. Gerhart, Barry. "Gender Differences In Current Starting Salaries: The Role of Performance, College Major, and Job Title." *Industrial and Labor Relations Review*. 43 (April 1990): 418-433.

   Analyzes salary differences in a private-sector firm based on gender. Discovers that most of the current differential can be attributed to differences in starting salaries between men and women. Although results are from one firm and cannot be projected to others, the findings support other research that asserts starting-salary differences are strong determinants of gender-based pay disparity. These differences, however, diminish as factors like performance on the job are factored in. Concludes that college major is also a key determinant of starting salary, and asserts that real or perceived barriers to certain occupations may factor into women's decisions about the major they choose.

270. Greene, Robert J. "Determinants of Occupational Worth." *Personnel Administrator*. 34 (August 1989): 78-80.

   Discusses three categories used to determine compensation of "occupational worth:" value to society or contribution to society's welfare; fair return on human resources; and economic value added as marginal contribution of labor to product value. Asserts that the three factors used in the Equal Pay Act of 1963 (skill, effort, responsibility, and working conditions) do not capture all the factors relevant to determining relative pay. Argues that other factors must be included in the "equation" before relative pay can be accepted by consensus as fair and just.

271. ---. "Is Gender Equality Advancing in the Workplace?" *American Economic Review.* 75 (May 1985): 262-278.

Contents: "Women Production Workers: Low Pay and Hazardous Work, by Janis Barry; "Executive Compensation: Female Executives and Networking," by Robin L. Bartlett and Timothy I. Miller; "Longitudinal Changes in Salary at a Large Public University: What Response to Equal Pay Legislation?" by Sharon Bernstein Megdal and Michael R. Ransom; "Sex Role Socialization and Labor Market Outcomes," by Mary E. Corcoran and Paul N. Courant.

272. Hill, M. Anne, and Mark R. Killingsworth, eds. *Comparable Worth: Analysis and Evidence.* Ithaca, NY: ILR Press, Cornell University, 1989.

Outlines the issues in the comparable worth debate, and offers current knowledge on its status.

273. Horner, Constance, and Patricia Schroeder. "Comparable Worth: A Wrong Turn." *Bureaucrat.* 16 (Winter 1987-1988): 4-9.

Summarizes the U.S. Office of Personnel Management's (OPM) report "Comparable Worth for Federal Jobs: a Wrong Turn Off the Road Toward Pay Equity and Women's Career Advancement." Congresswoman Patricia Schroeder offers opinions about OPM erroneous conclusions about comparable worth and the plight of women in the workforce; this argument is countered by Constance Horner, then Director of OPM.

274. Johansen, Elaine. "Comparable Worth: The Character of the Controversy." *Public Administration Review*. 45 (No. 5, 1985): 631-635.

Outlines and defines the major issues which characterize the comparable worth debate. Concludes that gender-based differentials in compensation still exist and delineates possible structural and organizational causes.

275. Lewis, Chad T., and Cynthia Kay Stevens. "An Analysis of Job Evaluation Committee and Job Holder Gender Effects on Job Evaluation." *Public Personnel Management*. 19 (Fall 1990): 271-277.

Through experiments with an evaluation committee, examines decisions about the worth of particular jobs based on knowledge of the gender of the incumbent. Concludes that, in fact, gender plays a significant role in the committee's determination of worth. Jobs that had female incumbents were valued less than jobs encumbered by males. Argues that anonymity of incumbents is one way to combat gender bias in job evaluation.

* Lewis, Gregory B. "Changing Patterns of Sexual Discrimination in Federal Employment." Cited above as item 209.

276. Lewis, Gregory B., and Mark A. Emmert. "The Sexual Division of Labor in Federal Employment." *Social Science Quarterly*. 67 (March 1986): 143-155.

Argues that sex segregation of General Schedule occupations, though decreasing, remains high. Estimates that almost 60 percent of all female federal employees would need to switch occupations to achieve complete occupational integration. Also discusses research results which show that male-dominated occupations provide higher salaries than those that are female-dominated, even when education, experience, race, sex, and veterans' preference are held constant. Concludes that occupational segregation explains one-third of the male-female earnings gap in the federal civil service.

277. Lewis, Gregory. "Sexual Integration of Occupations and Changes in Pay Inequality in Federal Civil Service." (unpublished, 1990).

Using data from the Office of Personnel Management's *Occupations of Federal White-Collar and Blue-Collar Workers*, examines the effect of occupational segregation in federal employment on wage disparity between male and female employees. Results show that the salary difference between the average male-dominated and female-dominated job is $3,800, or 16.6%. Women seem to do the best in these male-dominated occupations. Concludes, however, that jobs in federal white-collar employment have become more integrated over the last twenty years. Some explanation for this change can be attributed to women's increased qualifications, but a large portion can be attributed to different occupational choices and changing hiring and promotion practices.

278. Luna, Gaye. "Pay Equity and the Law: Where Women Stand in the Workforce." *Journal of Collective Negotiations in the Public Sector*. 20 (No. 3, 1991): 251-258.

Outlines legislative history and case law related to pay equity. Argues that employers and employees must do everything possible to advance wage and job equity. They must understand the law and identify potential areas of gender and gender-segregated pay disparities and voluntarily correct them by implementing the pay equity strategies outlined in the article.

279. Mangum, Stephen L. "Comparable Worth and Pay Setting in the Public and Private Sectors." *Journal of Collective Negotiations in the Public Sector.* 17 (No. 1, 1988): 1-12.

Asserts that pay equity continues to advance in public sector pay setting through collective bargaining, administrative decision, and the political process. Compares private sector pay setting mechanisms with those in the public sector and asserts that public sector job evaluation systems can be made consistent with comparable worth. Predicts more progress toward comparable worth in the public sector in the future.

280. Mann, M. "Pay Equity in the Courts: Myth vs. Reality. *Woman's Rights Law Reporter.* 8 (No. 1-2, 1984): 7-16.

Argues that pay disparity between men and women is the result of factors unrelated to discrimination in employment. Outlines legal history and asserts that sex segregation is due women's general lack of required qualifications for certain positions, lack of experience, and natural economic factors.

281. McGlen, N. E., and K. O'Connor. *Women's Rights.* New York: Praeger Publishing, 1983.

Opposes the establishment of legal and regulatory provisions which give extra resources (i.e., compensation) to "protected" groups. Views lack of parity in compensation as an outgrowth of low seniority and other market conditions.

282. Remick, Helen, ed. *Comparable Worth and Wage Discrimination: Technical Possibilities and Political Realities.* Philadelphia, PA: Temple University Press, 1984.

Discusses realities of wage discrimination related to occupational segregation and other structural barriers. Also outlines societal barriers and political climates which make economic parity so difficult to achieve. A comprehensive guide to all the issues.

283. Remick, Helen. "The Case of Comparable Worth in Washington State." *Policy Studies Review.* 5 (May 1986): 838-848.

Outlines cutting-edge comparable worth policies in the State of Washington. Argues that implementation of these policies has been painful and slow. Outlines policies related to the salary increases that will be given in Washington State over the next seven years. Concludes that, although Washington State was a pioneer in the area of comparable worth, and many valuable lessons can be learned from that particular experience, perhaps lessons about how *not* to implement comparable worth policies are more apparent.

284. Scholl, Richard W., and Elizabeth A. Cooper. "The Use of Job Evaluation to Eliminate Gender Based Pay Differentials." *Public Personnel Management.* 20 (Spring 1991): 1-18.

Responds to the recent debate that job evaluation systems have played a major role in maintaining disparities in male-female compensation. Analyzes two "generic" job evaluation systems vis-a-vis their effects on determining worth of male- and female-dominated jobs. Concludes that both the MIMA and Factor Evaluation (FES) systems can be as reliable as job-family based systems.

285. Scheibal, William. "*AFSCME v. Washington*: The Continued Viability of Title VII Comparable Worth Actions." *Public Personnel Management*, 17 (Fall 1988): 315-322.

Analyzes the 1985 comparable worth case, *The American Federation of State, County, and Municipal Employees (AFSCME) v. The State of Washington*, in which the original judgement was for the plaintiffs. Subsequently, that judgement was overturned. Discusses the resultant effect on comparable worth litigation as well as the legal history and current status of comparable worth.

286. Sorenson, Elaine. "Measuring the Pay Disparity Between Typically Female Occupations and Other Jobs: A Bivariate Selectivity Approach." *Industrial and Labor Relations Review*. 42 (July 1989): 624-639.

Controlling for individual choice to work and choice of occupation, concludes that women in female-dominated occupations earn 6-15% less than women in other occupations. Data from the 1984 Panel Survey of Income Dynamics are used to compare women with similar traits and characteristics in various occupations. Supports the theory that women are "crowded" into female-dominated occupations because of discrimination. This results in continued lower pay for women.

287. Steel, Brent S., and Nicholas Lovrich. "Comparable Worth: The Problematic Politicization of a Public Personnel Issue." *Public Personnel Management*. 16 (No. 1, 1987): 23-36.

Using examples from pay inequities in Washington State government and elsewhere, considers the salience of comparable worth and the pay equity issue. Examines the attitudes of women in the public service toward pay and compensation in the context of a highly charged political environment. Using data from employee surveys conducted in both the State of Washington and among federal employees, concludes that women are less likely to be dissatisfied with their pay than men. Discusses the future politicization of comparable worth, and asserts that certain assumptions are crucial to understanding the motivations of public employees.

288. Sylvester, Kathleen. "'Comparable Worth' Revisited: Whatever Happened After Washington State?" *Governing*. 1 (June 1988): 40-45.

Asserts that since it was decided in the 1983 Vinson case that Washington State had discriminated against thousands of women, several positive changes have occurred. Argues that concept of pay equity has received broader support, and that pay equity has become more than just another legal issue. Comparable worth is now on the agendas of state legislatures, city and county councils, and union negotiators who represent public-sector employees.

289. U.S. General Accounting Office. *Options for Conducting a Pay Equity Study of Federal Pay and Classification Systems; Report by the Comptroller General of the United States, March 1, 1985.* Washington: G.A.O., 1985. GAO/GGD-85-37, B-217675.

Two general approaches to evaluating pay equity in the federal civil service are discussed: economic analysis and job content analysis. Argues that both methods are valid and useful, and concludes that a federal pay equity study should incorporate both.

290. U.S. Office of Personnel Management. *Comparable Worth for Federal Jobs: A Wrong Turn Off the Road Toward Pay Equity and Women's Career Advancement.* Washington: G.P.O., 1987. (OPM Document 149-40-3.)

Argues that because of several factors, the condition and position of women in the federal government is good and quickly getting better. Further examines the concept of comparable worth in government, and concludes that although serious problems exist in the position classification and pay arena, a comparable worth system would not help women to advance more quickly in the federal civil service.

291. Vertz, Laura L. "Pay Inequalities Between Women and Men in State and Local Government: An Examination of the Political Context of the Comparable Worth Controversy." *Women & Politics.* 7 (Summer 1987): 43-57.

Discusses the political context of comparable worth through an analysis of pay inequities among men and women in state and local government.

292. Webster, George D. "Wage Discrimination: An Issue for the '80s." *Association Management*. 40 (August 1988): 224-225.

Delineates three approaches which have been proposed to close the wage gap: 1) Wait until women gain more experience and education and then move them up the ladder; 2) Use a comparable-worth approach and introduce a neutral job evaluation system; 3) Enforce laws that prohibit sex-based wage discrimination more strictly. Discusses Congressional action in this regard, as well as some legislation that has been proposed to do a study of pay-equity of the federal position classification system. At the state level, almost half of the states have or currently are studying their civil service systems for discriminatory pay practices, especially in female-dominated occupations.

293. Werwie, Doris M. *Sex and Pay in the Federal Government: Using Job Evaluation Systems to Implement Comparable Worth*. Westport CT: Greenwood Press, 1987.

Discusses theories of occupational segregation and the wage gap; historical development of the federal government's job evaluation (classification) system. Evaluates the factors, dimensions and operational indicators of the Factor Evaluation System (FES) and discusses why the FES is less beneficial to female-dominated jobs than was the old narrative classification system. Also discusses specific points in the development of the FES during which sex bias may have been injected. Reviews legal and legislative comparable worth issues as well as the history of the federal government's job evaluation system.

294. Wesman, Elizabeth C. "Unions and Comparable Worth: Progress in the Public Sector." *Journal of Collective Negotiations in the Public Sector.* 17 (No. 1, 1988): 13-26.

Cites major declines in union membership over the last several years, but points to Unions espousing comparable worth policies which are experiencing growth, albeit modest. Examines the role of Unions in comparable worth as well as legislative history and significant cases. Argues that involvement in the comparable worth issue may give Unions the shot in the arm they need.

295. Willborn, Steven. *A Secretary and a Cook: Challenges Women's Wages in the Courts of the United States and Great Britain.* Ithaca, NY: ILR Press, Cornell University, 1989.

A comparative analysis of comparable worth in the United States, Canada, Great Britain and throughout Europe. Explores both legal and practical differences related to comparable worth.

296. Winebrenner, Hugh. "The Implementation of Comparable Worth in Iowa. *Policy Studies Review.* 5 (May 1986): 863-870.

Describes and analyzes implementation of comparable worth policies in Iowa. Focuses on implementation of a job evaluation study mandated by the State Legislature, and implementation of the classification and compensation systems that were enacted based on the study conducted.

297. Wise, Lois Recascino. "Dimensions of Public Sector Pay Policies in the United States and Sweden." *Review of Public Personnel Administration.* 8 (Summer 1988): 61-83.

Discusses the compensation policies in the public sector in the United States and Sweden. Reports that in the US, with regard to "market power," the evidence suggests that the government does not offer competitive salaries to its employees. However, the concept of "fair treatment" between genders appears to exist. Discusses the government's reward system, where efforts are underway to create a performance-based reward system, with little success to date. In Sweden, pay comparability between public and private sector employees is rooted in the policy of "wage solidarity," but there has been slippage in the relative position of public sector employees. Asserts that Sweden has made significant progress in attaining equal wages between the sexes. Concludes that although the American and Swedish compensation models are very different, the results are very similar.

Pay Equity

RESOURCES

National Committee on Pay Equity (NCPE)
1126 16th Street, NW
Suite 411
Washington, DC 20036
(202) 331-7343

Provides information on all aspects of pay equity, speakers, grassroots assistance such as coalition building and strategy development, and access to a worldwide network of pay equity advocates.

Resources Which Can be Ordered from NCPE

1) *Raising Awareness About Pay Inequities.*

2) *Grassroots Action Kit.* Contains fact sheets, suggestions for organizing coalitions, working with the media and grassroots lobbying.

3) *Bargaining for Pay Equity: A Strategy Manual.* A how-to manual for developing and winning union pay equity campaigns.

Other Practical Guides on Pay Equity

1) *Strategies for Change: From Women's Experience to a Plan for Action.* Helps women's groups build strategies based on women's experiences using exercises. $9.00 plus $2.75 postage and handling outside Canada, $1.50 inside. Order from: Women's Research Centre, 101-2245 West Broadway, Vancouver, British Columbia, Canada V6K 2E4.

2) *Initiating Pay Equity: A Guide for Assessing Your Workplace.* Provides background on pay equity and guides users in making "an initial assessment of pay equity in your organization or jurisdiction." $6.00. Order from: Center for Women in

Government, University at Albany, S.U.N.Y. 302 Draper Hall, 1400 Washington Ave., Albany, NY 12222.

3) *Working for Pay Equity: A Blueprint for Local Community Action.* Describes eight years' experience with successful local pay equity campaigns by Women on the Job. $15.00. Order from: Women on the Job, 382 Main Street, Port Washington, NY 11050.

4) *The First Steps to Identifying Sex and Race Based Inequities in a Workplace: A Guide to Achieving Pay Equity.* Includes suggested strategies for showing that pay inequities exist in your workplace and numerous appendices that show how unions/organizations have used these strategies. $9.00, checks to "U.C. Regents." Order from: Labor Center, Institute of Industrial Relations, 2521 Channing Way, Berkeley, CA 94720.

5) *AAUW Pay Equity Action Guide* (#AAA63). $1.00. Order by mail: American Association of University Women Sales Office, 11722 Parklawn Drive, Rockville, MD 20852. Order by phone: 1-800-434-9991.

Equal Pay Act of 1963 -- Public Law 88-38
FAIR LABOR STANDARDS 29 SECTION 206

Prohibition of sex discrimination

(d) (1) No employer subject to any provisions of this section shall discriminate, within any establishment in which such employees are employed, between employees on the basis of sex by paying wages to employees in such establishment at a rate less than the rate at which he pays wages to employees of the opposite sex in such establishment for equal work on jobs the performance of which requires equal skill, effort, and responsibility, and which are performed under similar working conditions, except where such payment is made pursuant to (i) a seniority system; (ii) a merit system; (iii) a system which measures earnings by quantity or quality of production; or (iv) a differential based on any other factor other than sex: *Provided,* That an employer who is paying a wage rate differential in violation of this subsection shall not, in order to comply with the provisions of this subsection, reduce the wage rate of any employee.

CHAPTER 6

Mentors & Networking

"The situation of our youth is not mysterious. Children have never been very good at listening to their elders, but they have never failed to imitate them. They must, they have no other models." James Baldwin.

THE PROS & CONS OF HAVING CONNECTIONS

298. Bowen, Donald D. "Were Men Meant to Mentor Women?" *Training and Development Journal.* 39 (February 1985): 30-34.

Studies 32 mentor/protege relationships. Problems as well as advantages of mentoring are discussed. Argues that organizations should formalize and institutionalize mentoring programs.

299. Brass, D.J. "Men's and Women's Networks: A Study of Interaction Patterns and Influence in an Organization." *Academy of Management Journal,* vol. 28, no. 2, 1985: pp. 327-343.

Investigates interaction patterns of men and women in an organization and the relationship of these patterns to perceptions of influence and power, and promotions to management. Results show that individuals' positions in workflow and interaction networks relate strongly to their level of organizational influence. Women are rated as less influential than men, however, men and women show no differences on several of the measures used. Results also show that women are not well-integrated into men's networks including the organization's "dominant coalition." (Women whose immediate workgroups included both men and women were exceptions.) A follow-up study indicates that promotions were highly related to centrality in departmental, men's, and dominant-coalition work interaction networks.

300. Burke, Ronald J., and Carol A. McKeen. "Developing Formal Mentoring Programs in Organizations." *Business Quarterly* (Canada). 53 (Winter 1989): 76-79.

Argues that organizations can set up effective formal mentoring programs, but they must first answer several questions about organizational climate. Cites potential pitfalls to formal mentoring, and discusses balances that must be struck in male/female mentoring relationships.

301. Burke, Ronald J., and Carol A. McKeen. "Mentoring in Organizations: Implications for Women." *Journal of Business Ethics* (Netherlands). 9 (April/May 1990): 317-332.

Argues that mentoring is one high potential way to help women advance their careers. Unfortunately, women often lack access to information networks and the "norms" related to cross-gender relationships. Delineates problems with regard to managing cross-gender mentoring. These include sexual attraction, marital disruption, and damaging gossip. Recommends that organizations trying to establish mentoring programs should make the discussion of cross-gender mentoring an explicit part of the program. Articulates an agenda for research in mentoring, which includes: 1) an examination of the antecedents and consequences of mentoring, 2) the availability of mentors to women, 3) barriers to mentoring, and 4) the mentoring process and cross-gender mentoring.

302. Burshardt, S.C., and B. Allen. "Role Ambiguity in the Male/Female Protege Relationship." *Equal Opportunities International.* 7 (No. 2, 1988): 5-8.

Cites mentorship as an important element of career enhancement and growth. Argues that the male mentor/female protege combination seems to be the most complex of mentoring relationships because of the similarity between the cultural mating role and the mentoring role. This can lead to problems with peers and spouses. Strategies to overcome potential problems are given.

303. Campbell, Karen E. "Gender Differences in Job-Related Networks." *Work and Occupations.* 15 (May 1988): 179-200.

Examines differences in professional networks of men versus women. Relates this comparison to the analysis of gender-based occupational inequalities. Using data from men and women who recently changed jobs in four different white-collar occupations, discovers that 1) women know people in fewer occupations than men, 2) women's networks are negatively affected by having children younger than six years, and 3) women are more likely to change jobs in response to their spouses' mobility. Men's networks, on the other hand, do not seem to be affected by these phenomena.

304. Cannings, Kathy, and Claude Montmarquette. "Managerial Momentum: A Simultaneous Model of Career Progress of Male and Female Managers." *Industrial and Labor Relations Review.* 44 (January 1991): 212-228.

Analyzing data from a Canadian firm, discovers that men rely much more on informal networks than women, and that the networks men form are much more sophisticated and fully developed than women's. Women, in this case, seem to rely more on the meritocratic, formal systems to get promotions. And even though the women have better performance records, and formally bid for more jobs, men get more promotions per year of service than women.

305. Crouse, Janice Shaw. "The Managerial Woman: Settling In, Branching Out, Moving Up." *Vital Speeches.* 53 (No. 2, 1986): 57-60.

Outlines the situation faced by women in the workforce, and reasons why women still tend to hold lower level management positions and find it very difficult to break through to the top. Argues that, although there is still disparity in the treatment of men and women, attitudes are changing. Asserts that women must capitalize on their strengths and abilities; and an important aspect of this is to network to build contacts and alliances and let others know what they are achieving.

306. Darwent, Charles. "New Girls' Networks." *Management Today* (UK), January 1990, pp. 68-69.

A case study of a network formed London Business School (LBS) alumnae, called LBS Women. Argues that the small numbers of women in top-management jobs means that business women get little support from one another. Cites other such networks, some within specific industries and some more generic, but all with the central goal of mutual support. Points to an apparent paradox in that the women participating in the networks have already made their way past the "glass ceiling" barrier. Leaders of LBS Women assert that gathering women together to let them know that they are not alone may better enable them to deal with current problems and future changes.

307. Dreher, George F., and Ronald A. Ash. "A Comparative Study of Mentoring Among Men and Women in Managerial, Professional, and Technical Positions." *Journal of Applied Psychology.* 75 (Oct. 1990): 539-546.

Using survey data from 147 female and 173 male business school graduates, issues of backgrounds, organizations, positions, mentoring practices, compensation, and compensation satisfaction are explored. Results show that individuals who have extensive mentoring relationships report receiving more promotions, have higher incomes, and are more satisfied with their pay and benefits than individuals who have less extensive mentoring relationships. Results show no differences related to gender as far as frequency of mentoring, and gender does not seem to affect "mentoring-outcome" relationships.

308. Fagenson, Ellen A. "The Mentor Advantage: Perceived Career/Job Experiences of Proteges Versus Non-Proteges." *Journal of Organizational Behavior.* 10 (No. 4, 1989): 309-320.

Mentored and non-mentored men and women in high and low-level positions were asked to evaluate their level of satisfaction, career mobility/opportunity, recognition, security and promotion rate. Examines the extent to which these experiences varied as a function of their mentored status, sex, and organizational level. Results revealed that generally, mentored individuals report more satisfaction, career mobility and opportunity, recognition, and a higher promotion rate than non-mentored individuals.

309. Howard, Rosemary E., and Joan S. Munch. "Mentoring: A Federal Women's Program Initiative." *Bureaucrat.* 20 (Fall 1991): 13-14.

Highlights the Navy Medical Department's career mentoring pilot program which started in April, 1991. Through careful monitoring by the Federal Women's Program Managers as well as the use of several training sessions and organizational tools (e.g., the Myers-Briggs Type Indicator) to match mentors and proteges, the program appears to be quite successful. Contracts between mentors and proteges seem especially significant in this process because they clearly define the required commitment to the program for all participants.

310. McPherson, J.A. "Mobilizing the Mentor." *The Entrepreneurship Development Review.* 4 (Winter 1987): 18-19.

Discusses two approaches to assisting new entrepreneurs in accessing and using resources to plan, and manage new enterprise. Argues that community-based advisors of start-up entrepreneurs should adopt a networking approach rather than a hands-on mentoring approach, as a more efficient and effective means of counseling.

311. Mendelson, Jack L., A. Keith Barnes, and Gregory Horn. "The Guiding Light to Corporate Culture." *Personnel Administrator.* 34 (July 1989): 70-72.

Gives patterns and criteria from a successful corporate mentoring program, specifically Southland Corporation. Some criteria discussed include: minimal geographic distance between mentor and protege; minimal hierarchical distance--one level removed seems best; and early face-to-face contact between mentor and protege. Indicates that people who have mentors are generally more successful in organizations than people who do not.

312. Miller, J., J.R. Lincoln, and J. Olson. "Relationality and Equity in Professional Networks: Gender and Race as Factors in the Stratification of Inter-organizational Systems." *American Journal of Sociology.* 87 (1981): 308-35.

Examines conclusions from Weber's organizational principles of rationality and equity that organizational systems will neither create nor reinforce inequality based on gender or race. Using data from six multi-agency social service delivery systems, access to the networks of inter-organizational exchange that tied together the agencies in these systems was measured. This measure, called centrality, did not vary by race or gender. A complicated process of negotiation for resources and advantages, however was discovered--this phenomenon, it is argued, is not easily explained using classical organizational theory.

313. Noe, Raymond A. "Women and Mentoring: A Review and Research Agenda." *Academy of Management Review*. 13 (January 1988): 65-78.

Argues that the number of mentoring relationships does not appear to be keeping pace with the increasing numbers of women needing mentors. Cites studies which have shown that women who have mentors experience greater job success and job satisfaction than women who do not. Because there is a severe shortage of female mentors, and because men tend to hold more centralized, critical positions, a male mentor may be most valuable. Discusses barriers that may obstruct the development of mentoring relationships for women. Some of these include: lack of access to information networks, tokenism, stereotyping, socialization practices, and norms regarding cross-gender relationships. Concludes by setting forth an agenda for further research on mentoring relationships.

314. Paul, N. "Networking: Women's Key to Success." *Women in Management Review*, vol. 1, no. 3, 1985: pp. 146-151.

Asserts that networking is one viable way for women to overcome segregation in the workplace, as well as loneliness. A general guide to networking for women is included, along with descriptions of different types of networks, how they are structured, what they are and are not, and how they work.

315. Pazy, Asya. "Sex Differences in Responsiveness to Organizational Career Management." *Human Resources Management*, 26 (No. 2, 1987): 243-256.

Women are as effective as men on the job, yet they are promoted less. Argues that the "informal career management system" is an important resource in any organization, and it is currently under used by women to support career progression.

316. Ragins, Belle Rose. "Barriers to Mentoring: The Female Manager's Dilemma." *Human Relations*. 42 (No. 1, 1989): 1-22.

Asserts that the mentoring relationship is important for men, but it may be essential for women--especially female managers. Argues that mentors can buffer women from discrimination, and train female protegees in corporate politics. Discusses possible explanations for the infrequency of mentoring relationships among women in organizations including women not seeking mentors, and mentors not selecting female protegees.

317. Reich, Murray H. "The Mentor Connection." *Personnel*. 63 (No. 2, 1986): 50-57.

Reports on a study of female executives' experiences with mentoring, and compares the men and women to determine how important mentoring is to the advancement of women. Concludes that under optimum conditions, women benefit greatly from informal mentoring relationships.

318. Stern, Barbara B. *Is Networking For You? A Working Woman's Alternative to the Old Boy System*. Englewood Cliffs, NJ: Prentice-Hall, Inc., 1981.

Gives insights into the power of networking as a survival skill for working women. Networking systems enable women to know, use, and help each other in career advancing pursuits. Practical advice is given on setting up such networks.

319. Still, Leonie V., and Cecily Guerin. "Networking Practices of Men and Women Managers Compared." *Women in Management Review*. 2 (Summer 1986): 103-109.

Compares business, social and professional networking habits of Australian men and women executives. Finds that women are more likely than men to use networks to establish personal relationships, rather than to advance their professional careers.

320. Sussal, Carol M. "Group Work With Federal Employees." *Social Work With Groups.* 8 (No. 3, 1985): 71-79.

Discusses the use of short-term, lunchtime groups and suggests that they have broad topical appeal and multiple functions in a workplace setting. Such groups can provide a means for reaching out, can develop informal networks in a large bureaucracy, and may provide mutual aid. Describes a group program established for federal employees as part of the Federal Employee Counseling Service in New York City. Topics of various groups included returning to school, food abuse, assertiveness issues for women, and stress management.

* Vertz, Laura L. "Women, Occupational Advancement, and Mentoring: An Analysis of One Public Organization." Cited above as item 118.

321. Weiss, Rhoda. "Networking -- Getting Together to Get Ahead." *Healthcare Forum.* 29 (No. 1, 1986): 26-29.

Although the U.S. health care workforce is 80% female, men dominate management positions in a majority of hospitals. Women are entering the field in great numbers, but it could be decades before they play a more substantial role in the hospital environment. Shut out of traditional and informal "old boy" networks, women are organizing formal networks to aid in their search for career advancement. The American College of Healthcare Executives (ACHE) sponsors 16 such organizations. ACHE networks comprise top women managers and administrators. Membership usually is based on restrictive ACHE eligibility standards. The ultimate goal of these organizations is to help women move into positions of power and influence.

322. ---. "Women Finally Get Mentors of Their Own: More Female Advisers Are Guiding Young Women Executives Up the Ladder." *Business Week.* October 23, 1987, p. 74.

Discusses women helping women advance in their careers via mentoring. As more young women enter the workforce, more women have gone before them. It is argued that things can only get better for those who aspire to reach the top of their organizations. Larger numbers of mentors who happen to be women will help that cause.

ASSOCIATIONS & UNIONS

American Federation of Government Employees (AFGE)

80 F Street, NW
Washington, DC 20001
(202) 737-8700
John Sturdivant, President

Founded: 1932. Members: 250,000. Locals: 1300. AFL-CIO. Maintains a 400-volume library on labor law.

Publications: *Government Standard*, quarterly. Newsletter featuring AFGE news and legislative and regulatory information. Price: Included in membership dues. Circulation: 210,000. Convention/Meeting: triennial.

American Federation of State, County, and Municipal Employees (AFSCME)

1625 L Street, NW
Washington, DC 20036
(202) 452-4800
Gerald W. McEntee, President

Founded: 1936. Members: 1,200,000. Locals: 3000. AFL-CIO. Maintains library of 5,000 volumes. Committees: National Public Employees Organized to Promote Legislative Equality--PEOPLE. Absorbed: Black Employees of the Library of Congress (founded 1970).

Publications: *AFSCME Leader*, weekly. Covers public employee issues. Price: Included in membership dues. Circulation: 25,000. *Public Employee Newspaper*, 8/year. Journal covering pay equity for working women, the federal budget, day care, welfare reform, and other topics. Lists books and other resources for AFSCME activists. Price: Available to members only. Circulation: 1,100,000. *Women's Newsletter*, monthly. Also publishes *President's Letter*. Convention/Meeting: biennial.

American Foreign Service Association (AFSA)

2101 E Street, NW
Washington, DC 20037
(202) 338-4045
Sabine Sisk, Executive Director

Founded: 1924. Members: 9800. Associate membership is open to individuals and international organizations and corporations interested in foreign affairs, international trade, and economic policy. Conducts international conferences and symposia; holds monthly speaker programs. Administers award program for foreign service personnel and scholarship programs for foreign service dependents. Operates the Foreign Service Club; sponsors member insurance program. Bestows awards; operates speakers' bureau, and charitable programs.

Publications: *Directory of Retired Members*, periodic. *Foreign Service Journal*, 12/year. Magazine covering foreign policy and professional issues; includes book and periodical reviews, obituaries, and association newsletter. Price: $2.50/issue; $25/year. Circulation: 11,000.

The American Society for Public Administration

1120 G Street, NW, Suite 700
Washington, DC 20005
(202) 393-7878

Dues: Based on a sliding scale, from $55 to $80 per year; $35 for full time students.

ASPA is a nationwide nonprofit organization dedicated to improving management in the public service through the development and exchange of ideas, and through dissemination of information about public administration.

Civil Service Employees Association (CSEA)

PO Box 125, Capitol Station
143 Washington Avenue
Albany, NY 12210
(518) 434-0191
Joseph E. McDermott, President

Founded: 1910. Members: 220,000. Regional Groups: 6. Locations: 300. AFL-CIO. Members are state and local government employees from all public employee classifications. Negotiates work contracts; represents members in grievances; provides legal assistance for on-the-job problems; provides advice and assistance on federal, state, and local laws affecting public employees. Conducts training and education programs. Compiles statistics; conducts research.

Publications: *Newsletter*, periodic. *Public Sector*, biweekly. Convention/Meeting: annual.

Department of Defense Senior Professional Women's Association (DoD/SPWA)

P.O. Box 46560
The Pentagon
Washington, DC 20050
(703) 697-8979

Dues: $15 per year; $40 for three years.

The goal of DoD/SPWA is to encourage the advancement of women and to support their participation in policy and decision making at all levels in the Department of Defense. The DoD/SPWA presents opportunities for professional development, training, and networking. Their objective is to increase the number of women in mid-level and senior-level positions in the Department of Defense.

Federal Employees Coordinating Committee (FECC)

c/o Janet Garry
815 Connecticut Avenue, NW
Washington, DC 20006
(202) 463-8400
Janet M. Garry, Liaison

Founded: 1986. Members: 8. Organizations representing federal employees working in professional, managerial, and executive positions. Gathers and disseminates information regarding federal employee pay and benefits. Alerts members to congressional and administrative activities impacting federal employees.

Publications: *Inside Notes*, monthly. Newsletter offering guidance for effective lobbying on specific issues.

Federally Employed Women (FEW)

1400 I Street, NW Suite 425
Washington, DC 20005-2252
(202) 898-0994

Founded: 1968. Dues: $20 per year for chapter members; $30 for members-at-large.

Dedicated to removal of sex discrimination and the promotion of equality in the federal government. Maintains a legislative program with active grassroots networks. Provides career development and leadership training at national, regional, and local levels.

Publications: *FEW's News and Views*, Newsletter covering a wide variety of issues of import to women in the federal civil service; various reports, legislative agenda, and several booklets.

Federal Managers Association (FMA)

1000 16th Street, NW, Ste.701
Washington, DC 20036
(202) 778-1500
Paul E. Trayers, Executive Director

Founded: 1913. Members: 20,500. Regional Groups: 12. Local Groups: 140. Managers and supervisors in all federal agencies. Goals are to increase the efficiency of the work force, and to promote and support legislation beneficial to members. Examples of previous legislation that have benefitted members include: the retirement of federal employees with 30 years of service at age 55; the Supervisory (Wage Board) Job Grading Standards of 1968; increased government contributions to health and life insurance programs. Local groups sponsor seminars and training courses. Committees: Federal Management Institute; Political Action.

Publications: *Federal Management Journal*, quarterly. *Federal Manager*, monthly. *Federal Manager Quarterly*. Convention/Meeting: annual conference (with exhibits) - Washington, DC.

Federal Women's Interagency Board (FWIB)

PO Box 27621, Central Station
Washington, DC 20038
(703) 343-3098
Ana Villagra, Chairperson

Founded: 1971. Federal women's program managers and coordinators, equal employment opportunity employees, and others concerned with improving women's programs within the federal government. Aims to improve the status of federally employed women through federal programs. Seeks to make programs more effective, to widen opportunities for women, to elicit interest and support from management ranks, and to emphasize the employment needs of women and minorities. Provides legislative updates; sponsors mini-courses on topics such as career development and program management. Bestows awards.

Publications: *Federal Women's Interagency Board Directory*, annual. Also publishes *Barriers to the Employment and Advancement of Women in the Federal Government* and brochure. Convention/Meeting: monthly - always the third Wednesday of the month.

National Association of Government Employees (NAGE)

1313 L Street, NW
Washington, DC 20005
(202) 371-9108
Kenneth T. Lyons, President

Founded: 1961. Members: 195,000. Independent union of civilian federal government employees with locals and members in military agencies, Internal Revenue Service, Post Office, Veterans Administration, General Services Administration, Federal Aviation Administration, and other federal agencies, as well as state and local agencies. Activities include direct legal assistance, information service, legislative lobbying and representation, trained leadership in contract negotiations, employment protection, and insurance. Offers seminars; sponsors competitions; bestows awards. Maintains library of several hundred volumes of labor law, Title 5, and agency regulations.

Publications: *The Fednews*, monthly. Convention/Meeting: quadrennial.

National Association of Retired Federal Employees (NARFE)

1533 New Hampshire Avenue, NW
Washington, DC 20036
(202) 234-0832
H.T. Morrissey, President

Founded: 1921. Members: 510,000. State Groups: 53. Local Groups: 1700. Retired U.S. Government civilian and District of Columbia employees, their spouses, persons drawing annuities as survivors of retired U.S. government employees, present employees eligible for optional retirement, and federal employees with at least 5 years' service. Publications: *Retirement Life*, monthly. Magazine focusing on legislation and issues affecting federal civilian retirees and their dependents. Includes articles on annuities, government health benefits programs, and taxes. Offers legislative updates and statistics. Price: Included in membership dues. Circulation: 550,000. Convention/Meeting: biennial.

National Conference on Public Employee Retirement Systems (NCPERS)

311 Roosevelt Avenue
San Antonio, TX 78210
(512) 534-3262
Carlos Resendez, Secretary

Founded: 1942. Members: 425. National, state and local organizations whose purpose is to promote and safeguard the rights and benefits of public employees in retirement systems. Serves as congressional liaison. Conducts annual legislative workshop.

Publications: *Proceedings Record*, annual. *Word From Washington*, monthly. Convention/Meeting: annual - always April.

National Federation of Federal Employees (NFFE)

1016 16th Street, NW
Washington, DC 20036
(202) 862-4400
Sheila Velazco, President

Founded: 1917. Members: 52,000. Regional Groups: 9. Locals: 450. Independent. Opposes Social Security coverage for civil service workers. Conducts seminars on labor relations. Committees: NFFEPAC.

Publications: *Action*, monthly. *Federal Employee*, monthly. Also publishes promotional material. Convention/Meeting: biennial.

National Federation of Professional Organizations (NFPO)

PO Box 755
Sharon, CT 06069-0755
Wayne A. Nagel, President

Founded: 1967. Members: 12. Federal professional societies united to pool resources and cooperate on proposed legislation and executive developments affecting professional employees of the federal government.

National Treasury Employees Union (NTEU)

1730 K Street, NW, Ste. 1100
Washington, DC 20006
(202) 785-4411
Robert M. Tobias, President

Founded: 1938. Members: 145,000. Regional Groups: 16. Local Groups: 240. Employees of the federal government. Conducts research and educational training programs. Sponsors Federal Employee Educational Assistance Fund. Operates 3500 volume library. Committees: National Committee Resolutions; Treasury Employees Political Action. Absorbed: (1975) National Customs Service Association.

Publications: *NTEU Bulletin*, monthly. *NTEU Capital Report*, monthly. *NTEU Steward Update*, monthly. Convention/Meeting: biennial - August. Also holds annual legislative conference in February, Washington, DC.

Professional Development League (PDL)

c/o SEA
PO Box 7610, Ben Franklin Station
(202) 535-4323
Washington, DC 20044
Carol A. Bonosaro, President

Founded: 1981. Nonmembership: Participants are senior career executives of the federal government. Seeks to advance the professionalism of career federal executives through training and communications activities and research. Sponsors annual government ethics seminar and other seminars and conferences designed to enhance executive abilities of the federal government career administrator. Bestows awards for executive excellence.

Publications: Brochure. Convention/Meeting: annual training conference--always Washington, DC. Also sponsors luncheons and annual Distinguished Rank Award banquet.

Professional Managers Association (PMA)

PO Box 895, Ben Franklin Station
Washington, DC 20044
(202) 343-0883
Helene Benson, President

Founded: 1981. Members: 1000. Local Groups: 9. Federal civil service employees in mid-level management positions. Seeks to: improve the management, compensation, and public image of the federal work force; provide a vehicle for the advancement of interests and views of professional managers. Concentrates on issues affecting the interests of professional managers and their ability to efficiently conduct their duties. Issues include: insuring fairness of pay and appraisal systems; reversing the erosion of federal benefits; encouraging innovation in management practices. Conducts research on management issues; holds symposia.

Committees: Communication; Legislative Issues; Management Improvement.

Publications: *Professional Managers Association - Update*, bimonthly. Also publishes action memos, white papers, and brochure. Convention/Meeting: periodic.

Public Employee Department (of AFL-CIO) (PED)

815 16th Street, NW
Room 308
Washington, DC 20006
(202) 393-2820
Al Bilik, President

Founded: 1974. Members: 33. Affiliates representing a combined membership of 4,500,000 workers in federal, state, and local governments and the U.S. Postal Service. Involved with legislative, research, and communications activities at all levels of the public sector. Works closely with standing public employee committees of AFL-CIO state federations and local central bodies. Maintains library and provides information on all aspects of public sector labor relations. Bestows Golden Trough Award to a private contractor who has reneged or defaulted on a government contract. Compiles statistics.

Publications: *Issues and Answers*, 8/year. Newsletter. *PED Forum*, quarterly. Association and industry newsletter. Price: Free. *Privatization Update*, quarterly. Price: Free. Convention/Meeting: biennial.

Public Employees Roundtable (PER)

PO Box 6184, Ben Franklin Station
Washington, DC 20044-6184
(202) 535-4324
Joan Keston, Executive Director

Founded: 1982. Members: 88. Regional Groups: 5. Professional and management associations representing 950,000 public employees and retirees (30); government agencies are associate members (58). Promotes awareness of the contributions made by public employees by the quality of life of Americans. Encourages excellence, enthusiasm, and devotion in government; promotes public service careers. Sponsors Public Service Recognition Week the first week of May and the National Forensic League extemporaneous speech finals. Produces videos and public service announcements. Bestows awards and scholarships.

Publications: *The Public Eye*, 6/year. Price: Available to associate members only. *The Unsung Hero*, quarterly. Newsletter; includes facts and figures about civil service contributions. Price: Included in membership dues. Circulation: 8000. Also issues coloring book of careers in public service. Convention/Meeting: annual Associate Council members' meeting - always December or January.

Public Leadership Education Network (PLEN)

1001 Connecticut Avenue NW, Ste. 925
Washington, DC 20036
(202) 872-1585
Marianne Alexander, Director

Founded: 1978. Members: 14. A consortium of women's colleges working together to educate women for public leadership positions. Sponsors annual Women in Public Policy Seminar, Women and Congress Seminar, and public policy internships.

Publications: *PLEN Newsletter*, semiannual. Price: Free. Circulation: 1000. Also publishes *Learning to Lead* and *Wingspread Report: Educating Women for Leadership*. Convention/Meeting: annual public policy conference.

Section on Women in Public Administration (SWPA)

1120 G Street, NW Suite 700
Washington, DC 20005
(202) 393-7878

Dues: To join SWPA you must first be an ASPA member, SWPA dues are $17 per year.

SWPA works to develop programs and projects which promote the full participation and recognition of women in all levels and areas of public service.

Senior Executives Association (SEA)

PO Box 7610, Ben Franklin Station
Washington, DC 20044
(202) 535-4328
Carol A. Bonosaro, President

Founded: 1980. Members: 2500. Members of the Senior Executive Service and other supergrade executives and qualified GS-15s in the federal government. Seeks to: improve the efficiency, effectiveness, and productivity of the federal government; foster the professionalism of career federal executives; enhance public recognition of the contributions of federal career executives. Presents the concerns of SES leaders, the press, and the public. Testifies before congressional committees; issues fact statements and news releases. Initiates legal action to protect the interests of members.

Publications: *Action*, 10/year. Newsletter covering association activities and news affecting senior federal executives. Includes calendar of events and legislative updates. Price: Free to members; $45/year to nonmembers. Circulation: 2750. Convention/Meeting: annual conference (with exhibits) always held in Washington, DC.

Thomas Legal Defense Fund

PO Box 44364
Washington, DC 20026-4436
(703) 243-8479
Bernard Wiesman, President

Founded: 1971. Nonmembership: Locals 1534 and 1812 of the American Federation of Government Employees, representing employees of the foreign affairs agencies of the U.S. Government, Department of State, Agency of International Development, and U.S. Information Agency. Purpose is to protect the legal rights of employees of the foreign affairs agencies of the U.S. Government. Area of interest include income tax deductibility, age and sex discrimination, violation of civil service safeguards, alien spouse regulations, and recovery of legal fees.

Publications: Mailings and reports. Convention/Meeting: none.

Women In Municipal Government (WIMG)

c/o Don Jones
1301 Pennsylvania Ave. NW
Washington DC
(202) 626-3130
Don Jones, Coordinator

Founded: 1974. Members: 400. Women who are elected and appointed city officials including mayors, council members, and commissioners. Seeks to: encourage active participation of women officials in the organizational and policy-making processes and programs of the National League of Cities and state municipal leagues; identify qualified women for service in the NLC and other national positions; promote issues of interest to women and the status of women in the nation's cities.

Publications: *WIMG Update*, quarterly. Newsletter. Convention/Meeting: semiannual, with seminars and programs - always spring and fall.

CHAPTER 7

Women & Men

"There is more difference within the sexes than between them." Dame Ivy Compton-Burnett.

SIMILARITIES & DIFFERENCES

323. Brezina, Joan Turek, and Lucretia Dewey Tanner. "Top Men and Women View Public Service." *Bureaucrat.* 20 (Fall 1991): 29-32.

Using data from the Federal Executive Institute Alumni Association (FEIAA) annual survey, which looks at several general civil service employment issues, examines significant findings from 1990. These include: 1) The federal government appears to reward long, continuous service and longevity within an agency; 2) Few women are in executive or senior managerial ranks; 3) Those women who have achieved executive rank are better educated than their male counterparts; 4) Senior managers see little opportunity for advancement and women see even fewer opportunities; 5) The majority, both men and women, are satisfied with working for the federal government and their specific agency; and 6) Men and women alike are reluctant to encourage young people to pursue a career in public service.

*   Campbell, Karen E. "Gender Differences in Job-Related Networks." Cited above as item 303.

* Cannings, Kathy, and Claude Montmarquette. "Managerial Momentum: A Simultaneous Model of Career Progress of Male and Female Managers." Cited above as item 304.

324. Colwill, Nina L. "It's 1988 And There's a New Partnership." *Business Quarterly* (Canada). 53 (Fall 1988): 27-30.

Argues that there are more similarities between men and women than there are differences. Calls for changes on the individual level regarding the way we believe and voice stereotypes about the sexes. Suggests that buying in to stereotypes serves to perpetuate them.

325. Colwill, Nina L. "Men and Women in Organizations: Roles and Status, Stereotypes and Power." In *Working Women: Past, Present, Future*, ed. Koziara, K.S., Moskow, M.H., and Taner, L.D. Washington: Bureau of National Affairs, 1987, pp. 97-117.

Discusses societal relationships of sex roles, sex-stereotyping, status and power. Argues that historically, feminine traits have been viewed as inferior to masculine traits, and this has translated into employment discrimination. Reviews various stereotypical perceptions of men and women, and argues that these perceptions serve to disadvantage women in some job assignments and in managerial positions. Argues that sex stereotyping influences the power men and women have related to their jobs, and analyzes how men and women use power differently.

326. Daley, Dennis M. "Differing Perceptions Between Men and Women Over Personnel Management Practices: Gender-Related Differences Among Iowa Public Employees." *Public Personnel Management,* 13 (No. 3, 1984): 345-354.

Several items from the Federal Employee Attitude Survey (U.S. Office of Personnel Management, 1979), on organizational role, motivational factors, and performance appraisal systems were administered to 340 Iowa state employees to examine gender-related attitudes about personnel systems. Results show minor differences were between men and women, but for the most part, there is no evidence to support any "salient gender-related differences." Concludes that areas of future concern may focus on the perception of unrewarded performance that women are starting to develop.

327. Durand, Douglas E., and Leonard H. Chusmir. "When Men Manage Women." *Personnel*. 65 (April 1988): 62-64.

Outlines reasons why men typically manage women differently from the way they manage men. Barriers exist in both men's and women's minds, and these stereotypes serve to further disparate treatment. Issues of mentors, friends and relationships in the workplace, and special things women want from their managers and their jobs are discussed. Gives advice and guidance to male managers about managing women.

328. Filene, Peter J. *Him/Her/Self: Sex Roles in Modern America*. Baltimore: Johns Hopkins University Press.

Argues that sex role definition is changing very slowly, but that the "ideal" can be achieved, if society becomes more aware of the issues and effects of these definitions. Discusses how and why Americans define gender roles as we do.

329. Fine, Marlene G., Fern L. Johnson, and M. Sallyanne Ryan. "Cultural Diversity in the Workplace." *Public Personnel Management*. 19 (Fall 1983): 305-319.

Using survey data from a federal installation of 500 people issues related to organizational diversity are examined. Results indicate that organizational culture is different for women and minorities than it is for white men. Results also show that women and minorities view interpersonal, informal issues as barriers to their career advancement, while white men perceive that formal organizational structures have eradicated those barriers.

330. Forsythe, Sandra M. "Effect of Applicant's Clothing on Interviewer's Decision to Hire." *Journal of Applied Social Psychology.* 20 (November 1990): 1579-1595.

Examines the effect of applicants' clothing on interviewers' perceptions of management characteristics and decisions to hire women for management positions. Clothing masculinity significantly effected the interviewers' perceptions of the five management characteristics on which the applicants were rated. Applicants who wore more masculine clothing (e.g., a dark, tailored suit) received more favorable hiring recommendations than applicants wearing more feminine clothing (e.g., a soft beige dress).

331. Gold, Una O., and Judith K. Pringle. "Gender-Specific Factors in Management Promotion." *Journal of Managerial Psychology* (UK). 3 (No. 4, 1988): 17-22.

Explores comparative patterns of promotion for men and women managers and identifies factors that managers feel are significant in aiding or hampering their promotion. Finds significant similarity between the profiles of male and female managers, although female managers are given fewer promotions. Men and women perceive factors that aid similarly. These include: coaching by others, past training and experience, personal skill, and positive work attitudes. A major hindering factor for female managers is organizational attitudes toward women in a male-dominated environment. Concludes that female managers appear to carry an inequitable burden and are rewarded with fewer promotions.

332. Halas, Cecelia. *Why Can't a Woman Be More Like a Man.* New York: Macmillian, 1981.

Analyzes socialization patterns of women, and the resultant effects on their actions. Argues that these unique processes that women experience as girls leads to dependent, indecisive, and indirect manipulative behavior.

333. Harriman, Ann. *Women/Men/Management*. New York: Praeger Publishing, 1985.

Analyzes personal, social, and organizational influences that shape sexual identity and behavior and how sexual behavior affects organizational behavior, specifically sex discrimination in employment. Partial contents: The social-technological environment; The economic environment; Roles and stereotypes; Motivation and rewards; Leadership and power; Performance and perceptions of performance; Careers, career decisions, and career development.

334. Hartman, Bruce W., et al. "An Analysis of Gender Differences in the Factor Structure of the Career Decision Scale." *Educational and Psychological Measurement*. 47 (Winter 1987): 1099-1106.

Using a sample of college students (mostly freshman), applies the Career Decision Scale. Results show that most women experience indecision vis-a-vis careers based on their perceptions of external barriers. Most of the differences between men and women, however, are attributed to lack of information and knowledge about their own abilities and interests, as well as career options that exist.

335. Hollenbeck, John R., Daniel R. Ilgen, Cheri Ostroff, and Jeffrey B. Vancouver. "Sex Differences in Occupational Choice, Pay, and Worth: A Supply-side Approach to Understanding the Male-female Wage Gap." *Personnel Psychology*. 40 (Winter 1987): 715-743.

Although women still earn approximately 35% less than men, they make choices about which careers to pursue. Supply is defined as applicant's perceptions of the distribution of rewards available to them among different jobs and different employers. Demand is defined as employer's distribution of rewards among different jobs. Support is provided for the conclusion that occupational segregation is likely a major cause of the wage gap between men and women, but argues that some of the segregation is self-imposed by women. Makes the argument that sometimes women may feel underpaid, but not under-compensated since they still make choices about where to work.

336. Jaiprakash, Indira. "Women, Work and Work Commitment: A Review of Some Relevant Issues." *Indian Journal of Applied Psychology*. 23 (July 1986): 58-64.

Reviews various research into women's role in the workforce. Includes discussion of differences between men and women related to career decision-making, job-mobility, performance, motivation, sex segregation and sex stereotyping, and conflicts arising from competing roles that women play.

337. Lewis, Gregory B. "Men and Women Toward the Top: Backgrounds, Careers, and Potential of Federal Middle Managers." *Public Personnel Management*. (Forthcoming).

Examines salaries, occupational differences, education, mobility, managing of subordinates, relationships with supervisors, job satisfaction, and turnover rates among men and women in middle-management (i.e., GM-13 through GM-15) positions. Results show that women hold proportionately fewer middle-management jobs in the federal civil service than do men. Women earn less than men at this level, and they are less likely to have supervisory authority. (Some salary difference is explained by the greater seniority and education-level of men as a group.) Results also indicate that men and women handle problem employees in similar ways, but women seem to have more problems with their own supervisors. Women are more likely to attribute lack of advancement or reward to discrimination or a "buddy system."

338. Lewis, Gregory B. "Race, Sex, and Supervisory Authority in Federal White-Collar Employment." *Public Administration Review.* 46 (January/February 1986): 25-30.

Analyzes a one-percent sample of the Central Personnel Data File to determine if women and minorities are as likely to supervise employees and manage federal programs as their white male counterparts in the civil service system. Concludes that they are not, and that differences in age, education, and experience do not explain this phenomenon.

339. Lewis, Gregory B., and Kyungho Park. "Turnover Rates in Federal White-Collar Employment: Are Women More Likely to Quit Than Men? *American Review of Public Administration.* 19 (March 1989): 13-28.

Using a 1% sample of federal personnel records for 1976-86, reports that women's gross turnover rates were about one-third higher than men's in the federal civil service. These differences are often cited as a reason for hiring men over women for positions which have high training costs. Turnover rates are also commonly referred to as an explanation for pay disparity between men and women. Concludes that gross turnover rates can be misleading.

340. McCaney, M., S. Ahmed, et. al. "The Subjective Culture of Public Sector Women and Men Managers: A Common Instrumental/Expressive Value Orientation or, Two Different Worlds?" *Canadian Journal of Administrative Sciences.* 6 (June 1989): 54-63.

Study of male and female managers in the federal public service to determine if there are differences in the meanings of work values. Concludes that no significant differences related to gender exist. Implications for employment equity are discussed.

341. Metcalfe, B.P. "What Motivates Managers: An Investigation by Gender and Sector of Employment." *Public Administration*. 67 (Spring 1989): 95-108.

Studies attitudes of male and female managers from both the public and private sectors in Great Britain on what they want from their jobs and how they see their jobs meeting those needs. Concludes that there is little evidence to support the notion that women are less ambitious and career-oriented than men. Results also suggest that in both the public and private sectors, women have to make decisions with regard to marriage, family, and career that men do not appear to have to make.

342. Pave, Irene. "Dressing for Success Isn't What It Used to Be."*Business Week*. October 27, 1986, pp. 142-143.

Suggests that women now have a choice to deviate from more traditional, and more masculine dress. Women who reach the top of their organizations are in a position to deviate the most, or at least to be the most flexible about their dress, since others will probably take cues from them. Warns that individual corporate culture and common sense should not be forgotten, and suggests that women stick to wearing suits in more formal situations like making presentations.

343. Powell, Gary N. "Male/Female Work Roles: What Kind of Future?" *Personnel*. 66 (July 1989): 47-50.

Speculates about future changes to the lives of men and women in the workforce based on current trends. Argues that three "critical forces" will influence the roles men and women will play at work: equal opportunity--how the laws are enforced; socialization--how boy's and girl's socialization influences their occupational choices; and work and family issues--how employers help workers meet family responsibility, and how parents handle work-family balance.

344. Powell, Gary N. *Women and Men in Management*, Newbury Park, California: Sage Publications, 1988.

Discusses socialization, individual career choices, and recruitment vis-a-vis gender, as well as individual and organizational issues of gender that arise in the workplace. Gender stereotyping is discussed, as well as research related to sex differences in managerial behavior, commitment, motivation and stress. Argues that sex ratios in the workplace are one major determinant of sex stereotyping. Argues that there is little evidence to support the theory that men make better managers, and concludes that managers who are sex-neutral or androgynous are the most effective. Sex differences in career paths are also examined. Includes recommendations on how organizations can promote equal opportunity in employment.

345. Rizzo, Ann-Marie, and Carmen Mendez. "Making Things Happen in Organizations: Does Gender Make A Difference?" *Public Personnel Management*. 17 (Spring 1988): 9-20.

Through a series of workshops on gender-based differences in managerial behavior, concludes that women employ the same strategies as men to influence their subordinates, co-workers, and supervisors. Finds, however, that women do differ from men on assertiveness, and suggests that teaching women to use more assertive behavior will mitigate differences.

346. Rosenberg, Sheila. "Something in Common: Females Face the Same Challenges as Males When Climbing the Career Ladder." *Management World*. 16 (November-December 1987): 17-18.

Interviews conducted show that the barriers men and women face as they move through management are similar. Most of the 15 women interviewed reported support from associates and supervisors as a factor that was instrumental in their advancement. Argues that hard work and integrity are still the main ingredient to success for anyone.

347. Schmitt, Neal, and Scott A. Cohen. "Internal Analyses of Task Ratings by Job Incumbents." *Journal of Applied Psychology.* 74 (February 1989): 96-104.

Using survey data from 411 middle-level managers in 3 civil service occupational groups in state government on a task inventory using "time spent" and "difficulty" rating scales, two subsets of tasks are developed--general administrative and supervisory tasks. Results show that there were minor differences among respondents of different demographic subgroups, although differences related to occupational groups are significant. Gender differences resulted mainly from fewer women than men reporting that they were involved in tasks of a budgetary or financial nature and tasks that involved speaking or interacting with large groups of people outside the organization.

348. Scott, K. Dow, and Elizabeth McClellan. "Gender Differences in Absenteeism." *Public Personnel Management.* 19 (Summer 1990): 229-253.

Study of reasons why men and women secondary school teachers are absent from work. Confirms that women take more days off than men, but that "actual number of occurrences of women's absenteeism is not significantly greater" than men's. Similarities between men and women are also discussed; concludes that role conflict, number of dependents, and job involvement explain absenteeism for both sexes.

349. South, Scott J., et al. "Sex and Power in the Federal Bureaucracy; a Comparative Analysis of Male and Female Supervisors." *Work and Occupations*. 9 (May 1982): 233-254.

Tests Rosabeth Moss Kanter's hypothesis that sex differences in supervisory behavior result from sex differences in organizational power using survey data from 152 female employees and 46 supervisors in a large federal bureaucracy. Results show that female employees of female supervisors feel less job satisfaction than female employees of male supervisors. Female employees of female supervisors also report lower group morale, and are more likely to describe their supervisor as "controlling and particularistic." With regard to differences in organizational power (measured using an index of supervisor's job status, the amount of say they believe they have in their superior's decisions, and the amount of autonomy they feel they have on the job), female supervisors perceive that they have less than their male counterparts in the context of their organizations.

350. Stivers, Camilla. "Toward a Feminist Perspective in Public Administration Theory." *Women & Politics*. 10 (No. 4, 1990): 49-65.

Argues that the field of public administration lacks a feminist perspective; raises the issue of women's exclusion from public administration theory and topics and questions neglected as a result. Four important issues are suggested as areas where a feminist perspective might offer fresh insights: the question of administrative knowledge; the model of the ideal public servant; the nature of administrative discretion; and the dimensions of the administrative state.

351. Suojanen, Waino W. "The Emergence of the Type E Woman: How Does the Female Manager React to the Demands of the Business World?" *Business: The Magazine of Managerial Thought and Action*. 37 (January/March 1987): 3-7.

Studies female executives' reactions to the stresses and demands of work life compared with those of her male counterpart. Partial contents: The Work Place and Type A Behavior in Women; Coronary Heart Disease in Type A Women; A New Pattern--The Multidimensional Woman.

352. Sutton, Charlotte Decker, and Kris K. Moore. "Executive Women: 20 Years Later." *Harvard Business Review: The Magazine of the Thoughtful Manager.* 63 (September/October 1985):42-44.

Compares the results of a 1985 follow-up survey of 1,900 male and female American executives. The 1985 results are compared with results from a 1965 survey, and attitudes of men and women executives are compared.

353. ---. "Sex Differences in Support for Organizational Advancement." *Work and Occupations.* 14 (May 1987): 261-285.

Using a sample of 486 male and 356 female employees of a large federal bureaucracy, explores the differences in support men and women receive as they advance in organizations. Reports on perceptions of men and women about the social support they receive from four sources: male peers, female peers, male supervisors, and female supervisors.

COMMUNICATION BETWEEN WOMEN AND MEN

*   Cohen, Lynn Renee. "Nonverbal (Mis)Communication Between Managerial Men and Women." Cited above as item 226.

354. Hodgson, Richard C., and Eileen D. Watson. "Gender-Integrated Management Teams--Part I," *Business Quarterly* (Canada). 52 (Fall 1987): 68-72.

Calls for gender-integrated management training as one way to facilitate integrated management teams. Illustrates social and communication problems that arise when women and men work together at higher levels in an organization. Argues that positive action must be taken to foster change at the personal, professional (i.e., work relationships), and corporate levels.

355. O'Donnell, Holly. "Leadership Effectiveness: Do Sex and Communication Style Make a Difference?" *English Journal.* 74 (March 1985): 65-67.

Analyzes communication styles related to managers' gender and perceived effectiveness. Outlines ways to increase awareness of communication issues in young people. Activities suggested include: class discussion, interviews with community leaders for opinions on female leadership, and listing common characteristics of female executives.

356. Parlee, Mary Brown. "Getting a Word in Sex-Wise." *Across the Board.* 21 (September 1984): 7-10.

Discusses the effects of some women's communication style on their credibility in the workplace. Many women, it is argued, use inflections when speaking, talk faster than their male counterparts, and use qualifiers and questioning intonations. Research shows that women also maintain eye contact more than men, smile more when speaking, and nod frequently. Women in executive positions try to combat this phenomenon by speaking more slowly and more loudly to give a more "businesslike" impression.

357. Tannen, Deborah. *You Just Don't Understand: Women and Men in Conversation.* New York: Morrow, 1990.

Outlines the differences as well as the sources of those differences between the way women and men communicate. Argues, through research which is illustrated by anecdotes, that men tend to seek respect and independence, while women want to feel connected and be liked by others. Concludes that, as a result of these basic differences, communication between men and women can be like cross-cultural communication.

358. Smeltzer, L.R., and J.D. Werbel. "Gender Differences in Managerial Communication: Fact of Folk-Linguistics?" *Journal of Business Communication.* 23 (No. 2, 1986): 41-50.

Using data from a study of female and male MBA students, the issue of differences in communication related to gender is examined. The stereotypical communication style of women is verbose language, laden with indirect questions and limited vocabulary. Concludes that stereotypes are inaccurate since no differences seem to exist in the written communication of male and female participants.

CHAPTER 8
Training

"Training is everything. The peach was once a bitter almond; cauliflower is nothing but cabbage with a college education." Mark Twain.

GENERAL

359. Boesel, Andrew. "Federal Training Opportunities." *Bureaucrat*. 16 (Spring 1987): 40-41.

Argues that although budgets are tight, training opportunities are available in the federal government if one actively seeks them out. Outlines training opportunities open to federal employees, including highly structured classroom opportunities as well as individual, ad hoc efforts. Claims that efforts to identify and train future managers in the government have been lacking, and recommends that young professionals seek involvement in professional associations to gain experience in positions of leadership.

* Brunet, Jean, and Serge Proulx. "Formal Versus Grass-Roots Training: Women, Work, and Computers." Cited above as item 68.

360. Diener, Thomas, and Otis Holloway Owens. "Preparing Women and Minorities for Educational Research and Leadership: A Case Study." *Journal of Negro Education*. 53 (Fall 1984): 491-498.

Describes the strategies and activities of the University of Alabama's Project Growth. This project demonstrated that, with encouragement and training, women and minorities could become more visible, could be appointed to positions challenging the upper limits of their skills, and could be more productive as educational researchers.

361. Fitzgerald, Patricia A. "Meeting the Needs of Women Managers: The UNB Training Programme." *Journal of Management Development* (UK). 8 (No. 6, 1989): 49-54.

Describes a 1987 University of New Brunswick executive training program for women. Research on the needs of women managers who wanted more mobility is outlined. Results indicate that these women felt that they had fewer available role models and were more isolated on the job than their male counterparts, received less feedback and progressed more slowly. Three key issues for women managers are identified: 1) women who are promoted to upper management often perceive that they lack important technical skills, 2) women face demands in society and must develop strategies that allow them to be successful, and 3) the greatest problems for women in the workplace frequently arise because of faulty perceptions and unrealistic expectations.

362. Hammond, Valerie. "Management Training for Women." *Journal of European Industrial Training* (UK). 10 (No. 7, 1986): 15-22.

Argues that women have often been overlooked for formal training programs. Asserts that employers need make sure that they are including women in training for subject-matter specific and general management skills. Outlines training research which has indicated that training programs for women should include: 1) gaining an awareness of the political and cultural aspects of organizations; 2) identifying and building a personal management and leadership style; 3) communication skills, 4) self-management, (e.g., time management and stress management; and 5) career/life planning.

363. Harlan, Sharon, and Ronnie Steinberg, eds. *Job Training for Women: The Promise and Limits of Public Policies.* Philadelphia, PA: Temple University Press, 1989.

Analyzes and reviews the public education system and job training in the United States vis-a-vis their effectiveness for women.

* Hodgson, Richard C., and Eileen D. Watson. "Gender-Integrated Management Teams--Part I." Cited above as item 354.

364. Howell, Ruth S., and Helen Schwartz. "Community-Based Training for Reentry Women in Nontraditional Occupations." *New Directions for Continuing Education.* Fall 1988, pp. 65-77.

Discusses community-based organizations that provide special training services and opportunities to women in nontraditional careers.

365. Hoy, Judith. "Skills of Women Needed at the Top." *Executive Excellence.* 7 (No. 6, 1990): 14-15.

Argues that women tend to possess the ability to build effective relationships with co-workers and with customers. This skill is crucial to achieving quality and leadership in organizations. The ability to listen, to resolve conflict, and to get people to work together are skills which women are more likely to have than are men. Argues that solutions to "business problems" lie in being willing to look at the relationships in the organization. Avers that organizations need to encourage everyone to develop the skills of building relationships by appreciating and using the skills that women often bring to the workplace.

366. Lewittes, Hedva J., and Sandra Lipsitz Bem. "Training Women to Be More Assertive in Mixed-Sex Task-Oriented Discussions." *Sex Roles: A Journal of Research.* 9 (May 1983): 581-96.

Analyzes a sample of female undergraduates with low participation levels in mixed-sex conversation. Participants received training in assertiveness. Changes in behavior resulted from the training, and suggested that the lack of assertiveness while in the presence of men, rather than lack of knowledge, inhibited women's participation in discussions.

367. McCall, Morgan W., Michael M. Lombardo, and Ann M. Morrison. "Great Leaps in Career Development." *Across the Board.* 26 (No. 3, 1989): 54-61.

Argues that employees cannot be fully developed unless and until they take on assignments that are new, challenging, and different from their familiar area of expertise. Assignments that seem "too tough to handle" are just the opportunities that serve to develop and advance employees. Using interview data from 191 corporate executives, developmental experiences that have made lasting changes are described.

368. Newell, Terry. "The Future of Federal Training." *Public Personnel Management.* 17 (Fall 1988): 261-271.

Argues that training in the federal government over the next 10-15 years will be crucial because of several factors, and that a large investment in training will be imperative. Since the baby-boom has ended, there is a demographic shift at work which has decreased the number of entry-level workers, and increased the number of middle-aged workers. Argues that the government is also rapidly losing many skilled, experienced workers, and technological change will necessitate more technology training and shifts in organizational behavior. Concludes that future training outfits will need new delivery sites, new delivery methods, and new structures, roles, and skills of training staff to meet the new demands of the workforce.

369. Newland, Chester A., and David A. Turner. "Executive Training Fundamentals: Training Priesthood Abandoning Necropolis." *Bureaucrat.* 17 (Spring 1988): 15-17.

Discusses three fundamentals that should be acknowledged in the design and implementation of executive training in the federal government: professional and civic networking, limited in-house training, and executive responsibility. Argues that, although the U.S. Office of Personnel Management's training programs were lacking during the Reagan Administration, some good things resulted. Cites the Management Excellence Inventory (MEI), which unfortunately, was not used. Argues that any complete training program for executives must serve to link top executives with agency training programs, and managers in the public and private sectors. Concludes that this will require a new paradigm for traditional trainers who will try to maintain the status quo.

370. Stark, Elizabeth. "The Making of a Manager." *Psychology Today* 21 (August 1987): 28-32.

Describes a 3-day workshop held for women executives. Lectures focused on stress, goal setting, and information sharing between participants. Group exercises emphasized decision making and cooperation. Psychological and abilities tests were administered and feedback on personal characteristics was given to help participants define success and strategize about how to achieve it.

371. Taylor, Patricia A. "Institutional Job Training and Inequality." *Social Science Quarterly.* 66 (March 1985): 67-78.

Using the U.S. Civil Service as a case study, the relationship of institutional job training to salary is examined by minority, sex, and by time in the career. Results suggest that job training is especially important to employees early in their careers; and that minorities and women receive less training than white males.

372. Taylor, M. Susan, and Christina M. Giannantonio. "Participants' Reactions to Special Assignment Programs: Favorability and Predictors." *Public Personnel Management.* 18 (No. 4, 1989): 430-439.

Examines reactions of participants to a 20-year-old special assignment program in the federal government. Concludes that the program under investigation is beneficial to most participants. Argues that special assignment programs have long been thought an effective means to create opportunities for and advance the careers of talented individuals.

373. Turner, Yolanda, and Karen Clark-Schock. "Dynamic Corporate Training for Women: A Creative Arts Therapies Approach." *Arts in Psychotherapy.* 17 (Fall 1990): 217-222.

Presents four case studies from an art therapy workshop. The workshop is designed for women to heighten self-awareness. Techniques are used for effective conflict resolution, stress management, and directedness. The training includes lectures, group discussion, assessment instruments, and art/movement tasks. The workshop allows women to experience credit-robbing mannerisms in body attitude and behaviors that empower and project a strong sense of self.

374. Vaughan, Edward, and Barbara Lasky. "How Will Women Manage? A Speculation on the Effects of Equal Opportunities in Management Training." *Journal of General Management.* 16 (Summer 1991): 53-65.

Discusses and analyzes the Social Justice model of discrimination which asserts that discrimination against women in employment practices is a violation of some of the basic human rights laid out in the United Nation's 1948 Universal Declaration of Human Rights and the 1966 International Covenant on Civil and Political Rights. Argues that the Social Justice model has set itself apart from the other major models supporting equal employment training opportunities for women, specifically the Human Capital model.

375. Wolf, Dona. "Revitalizing Federal Training and Development." *Bureaucrat.* 20 (Summer 1991): 19-22.

Outlines the U.S. Office of Personnel Management's (OPM) revitalized plan to offer training to the federal workforce. Cites the new organization that OPM has created to create policy for and administer the government's human resources development. Articulates a new philosophy embedded in federal training which emphasizes training other than traditional classroom training--i.e., a wide spectrum of learning experiences that will prepare the workforce for meeting the future demands of their jobs. Argues that training and development opportunities and programs must update and expand federal employee's skills and experiences as they move along their career paths.

FEDERAL TRAINING RESOURCES

Information listed below comes from the U.S. Office of Personnel Management's Human Resources Development Group Training guides.

LEGIS Fellows Program

Program Elements
The LEGIS Fellows Program was established in 1979 as a developmental activity primarily for executives and candidates in the Senior Executive Service and for managers in agencies' development programs. The Program provides assignments for personnel whose current or prospective positions may require working knowledge of the operations of the Congress. The Fellows receive instruction and hands-on experience in a congressional office through training/developmental activities consisting of three (3) weeks of intensive briefings on the operations and organization of the Congress; an assignment, full time, on the staff of a Member, committee, or support agency/organization of the Congress in Washington, D.C., and frequent seminars during the work assignment on Capitol Hill. For some agency personnel (e.g., management/executive development and SES personnel), the Program will provide training essential to their individual development plans.

During FY 1992, the Program will include (a) two sessions which are six months long, beginning in January and in June; (b) one full-year session, beginning in January and ending in December, 1992. Each session includes a three-week orientation, the opportunity for Fellows to seek and obtain a full-time assignment for the duration of the Fellowship, and frequent seminars.

Participant Qualifications
Approximately 30 Fellows will be selected for each six-month class. Projected enrollment for full-year class is 10-15 Fellows. Nominee qualifications include: minimum grade of GS/GM-14 or equivalent (in special circumstances, participants at the GS/GM-13 may be accepted)

and at least two years of Federal service in the Executive Branch; demonstrated flexibility in work habits; ability to work in an unstructured environment; ability to initiate work independently with minimum supervision, direction or assistance; and an interest in legislative procedures, practices and techniques. Preferred nominees are members of the Senior Executive Service, SES Candidates and other personnel designated for executive development.

Information and Nominations:

Office of Personnel Management
Long-Term Development Programs
Box 164
Washington, DC 20044
ATTN: Director, LEGIS Fellow Program
Telephone: (202) 632-3282

Women's Executive Leadership Program

The Women's Executive Leadership (WEL) Program is a developmental program that provides supervisory/managerial training and development opportunities for high-potential Federal employees preparing them for future positions as supervisors and managers.

Designed for non-supervisory women and men or new supervisors with less than one year's supervisory experience during their Federal careers who are at the GS-11 or GS-12 level, the WEL Program is tailored to the participant's own developmental needs focusing on those competencies and effectiveness characteristics needed to be a successful supervisor or manager.

Under the direction of the U.S. Office of Personnel Management's Office of Executive and Management Development, the WEL Program is to be completed in twelve months. The WEL Program is open to regional as well as local employees, but all required training will take place in the Washington, DC metropolitan area and surrounding residential training sites.

Information
For more information, please contact the Women's Executive Leadership Program on 202-632-5109 or FTS 8-632-5109.

Executive Potential Program

The Executive Potential Program is a career enhancement program that provides training and developmental experiences for high potential individuals GS/GM 13-14--that prepare them for managerial and executive positions in the Federal government.

Designed primarily for occupational specialists at the journeyman level who are transitioning into management as a second profession, the Program holds special significance for employees who need to complement their technical expertise with professional management skills. The Executive Potential Program provides a foundation of management training and appropriate developmental experiences leading to candidacy in other management and SES development programs.

Under the direction of the Office of Personnel Management's (OPM) Human Resources Development Group (HRDG), the Program will be completed in 12 months. The Program is open to all field and Washington, DC employees. Four of the five required training sessions will take place outside the DC metro area, but within a 300-mile radius of Washington, DC. The fifth and final session will take place in Washington, DC. Departments and agencies will be responsible for all travel and per diem costs for participant attendance at training.

General Program Design
A structure has been designed for program participants (who have been nominated by their department or agency as having demonstrated exceptional managerial/executive potential) to acquire or enhance the competencies and effectiveness characteristics needed to become successful Federal managers.

Program Components
1. Orientation
2. Individual Needs Assignment
3. Individual Development Plan
4. Senior Advisors
5. Core Training Curriculum
6. Developmental Work Assignments
7. Cluster Group Participation
8. Agency Program Coordinators

Participant Qualifications
The program is limited to career/career conditional full-time permanent employees, GS/GM 13-14, who have demonstrated significant managerial/executive potential. Participants may be at the entry level of management, but may have had limited formal managerial training. They may soon be expected to assume responsibility for programmatic or policy leadership in their agencies.

Information and Assistance
OPM's Human Resources Development Group, Office of Executive and Management Development manages the Program and works closely with department and agency executive development program coordinators and participants to insure integration of the Program with their human resource development needs. For more information, contact the Executive Potential Program staff at:

U.S. Office of Personnel Management
Executive Potential Program, Room 308
P.O. Box 164
Washington, DC 20044
Phone: 202-632-5109

THE MANAGEMENT SEMINARS

Seminar For New Managers
This seminar provides new government managers with an opportunity to learn and practice managerial skills needed to effectively meet the current and future challenges of public service. The purpose of the seminar is to assist participants in making the transition to their new management position. Personal assessments, small group analyses, interactive learning methods, and case examination help participants master the complex demands of their new roles.

Audience: Public sector managers with less than two years of managerial experience. Participants will normally be at the GM/GS 13 level, but the seminar is also open to new members at higher grades. New managers at the GS 12 level may also be accepted with prior OPM approval and upon certification of special need or circumstance by the nominating agency.

Management Development Seminar
This seminar provides an opportunity for experienced managers to develop new capabilities as well as enhance those which have supported their management excellence in the past. The purpose of this seminar is to assist managers and executives in achieving continuous organizational improvement. It provides information on trends affecting management behaviors and processes and current developments in the following areas:

* Public Service Environment

* Leadership and Organizational Dynamics

Audience: Successful experienced managers. Participants will normally be at the GM/GS 14 and 15 levels, though high-performing nominees at the GM/GS 13 level are welcome.

Executive Development Seminar

This intensive seminar assists senior managers in making the transition to executive positions. The seminar provides a working knowledge of executive roles in government and helps participants develop, practice and expand their executive leadership skills. Briefings, case studies, simulations, small team projects and individual study are used to provide a diversified executive-level developmental experience.

Audience: The Executive Development Seminar meets the government-specific need for SES candidate development. Because it is keyed to effectiveness characteristics and functions associated with success at the executive level, the seminar is appropriate for GM/GS 15's as well as recently-appointed members of the Senior Executive Service. High-performing GM/GS 14's who are in executive development programs may also be nominated.

Seminar on Managerial Competencies

This seminar emphasizes management skills needed to operate in the policy context typical of many higher-level management jobs.

The program is designed with two core objectives: (1) to build skills in developing effective working relationships and collaborative problem-solving; (2) to increase ability to analyze complex management and policy issues.

The seminar makes extensive use of experiential learning techniques: simulations, team building exercises, and case studies. The case materials used are drawn from real experiences of government managers managing programs, and planning and implementing public policy.

Audiences: Managers and executives who have moved from technical, scientific, or specialist positions directly into management at a relatively high level, without benefit of supervisory and management experience and training at lower levels. Participants should be at the GM/GS 14 level and above.

The Senior Executive Service Candidate Development Program
Provides all formal training needed to meet the requirements of the Qualifications Review Board for SES candidates. This training includes the 2-week Washington Executive Seminar and four different 3-day seminars. This program is limited to persons in SES candidate programs, incumbent SES members, and high potential GS/GM 15 employees.

The Management Development Centers
OPM's Management Development Centers, formally Executive Seminar Centers, are a unique interagency training and development resource for middle level Government managers. The Centers provide a core management curriculum which addresses the competencies, skills, and abilities needed by Federal managers at the full performance mastery level and supports the transition from manager to executive. The Centers also provide a wide range of professional development programs dealing with public management and national policy issues. All these programs are conducted in a residential setting. Most of the Centers' programs have been evaluated by the American Council on Education and have been certified for graduate level credit at cooperating universities around the country.

The Federal Executive Institute
The Federal Executive Institute (FEI) was established in 1968 as an interagency residential executive development center focused on the generalist role of the senior government executive. The Institute's programs assume that senior officials are already highly skilled individual agencies. As a result, FEI programs are focused on broadening experiences required when managers emerge from the rather narrow loci of their own specializations to enter a new and second profession for which most have never received formal training--as leaders and Federal career executives. These Senior Executive Service members and selected GS/GM 15's are competitively selected by their agencies to attend the 4-week program (Leadership for a Democratic Society), 1-week Work-Team Development programs, or short custom-designed, agency-specific strategic planning sessions. For further information, write or call:

Training 181

The Federal Executive Institute
Office of Personnel Management
1301 Emmet Street
Charlottesville, VA 22901
Commercial: (804) 980-6200
Fax: (804) 979-1030

Regional and Washington, DC, Training Centers
OPM has training centers in each of its five regions and in Washington, DC. Each of the five Regional Training Centers provides the full range of OPM training and development services. For information contact the OPM Training Center servicing your department or agency location:

Atlanta Regional Training Center
Office of Personnel Management
Richard B. Russell Federal Building
75 Spring Street, S.W.
Atlanta, GA 30303-3109
Commercial: (404) 331-3488
Fax: (404) 331-3331

States served: Alabama, Florida, Georgia, Mississippi, North Carolina, South Carolina, Tennessee, and Virginia.

Chicago Regional Training Center
Office of Personnel Management
John C. Kluczynski Federal Bldg.
230 S. Dearborn St., 30th Floor
Chicago, IL 60604-1687
Commercial: (312) 353-2919
Fax: (312) 353-3297

States served: Illinois, Indiana, Iowa, Kansas, Kentucky, Michigan, Minnesota, Missouri, Nebraska, North Dakota, Ohio, South Dakota, West Virginia, and Wisconsin.

Dallas Regional Training Center
Office of Personnel Management
1100 Commerce Street, Room 4F25
Dallas, TX 75242-9968
Commercial: (214) 767-8245
Fax: (214) 767-8205

States served: Arkansas, Arizona, Colorado, Louisiana, Montana, New Mexico, Oklahoma, Texas, Utah, and Wyoming.

Philadelphia Regional Training Center
Office of Personnel Management
Wm. J. Green, Jr., Federal Building
600 Arch Street, Room 3406
Philadelphia, PA 19106-1596
Commercial: (215) 597-2527
Fax: (215) 597-8613

States served: Connecticut, Delaware, Maine, Maryland, Massachusetts, New Hampshire, New Jersey, New York, Pennsylvania, Puerto Rico, Rhode Island, Vermont, and Virgin Islands.

San Francisco Regional Training Center
Office of Personnel Management
120 Howard Street, 2nd Floor
San Francisco, CA 94105
Commercial: (415) 744-7280
Fax: (415) 744-7311

States served: Alaska, California, Hawaii, Idaho, Nevada, Oregon, Pacific Ocean Area, and Washington.

Washington Training and Development Services
Office of Personnel Management
P.O. Box 7230
Washington, DC 20044-7230
Commercial: (202) 632-6028
Fax: (202) 632-5602

Area served: The Washington, DC, Metropolitan Area.

CHAPTER 9

Women in Non-Traditional Occupations

"Nil corborundum illegitimi." Anonymous

376. Allison, Maria T., and Margaret C. Duncan. "Work, and Leisure: The Days of Our Lives." *Leisure Sciences.* 9 (No. 3, 1987): 143-161.

Analyzes the nature of "flow" and "antiflow" by looking at 8 professional and 12 blue-collar women's experiences at work and outside work. "Antiflow" is characterized by boredom, frustration, and anxiety-- "flow" is the antithesis. Results suggest that professional women experience "flow" both at work and outside work, while blue-collar women tend to experience "flow" only outside work. Both groups experienced some "antiflow" when they performed tasks that were repetitious, tedious, and simplistic, regardless of whether the setting was white- or blue-collar. Such repetitive, tedious tasks are a small part of professional jobs analyzed, but a fairly large part of blue-collar jobs.

377. Armor, David J., and David J. Shea. *Task Force on Women in the Military.* Washington: U.S. Office of the Assistant Secretary of Defense, 1988.

In this Feb. 2, 1988 news briefing, Principal Deputy Assistant Secretary of Defense for Force Management and Personnel and Director,

Directorate of Information, U.S. Dept. of Defense, discuss the role of women in the military. Policy Initiatives examined deal with sexual harassment, quality of life and combat exclusion.

*   Arriola, Elvia R. "'What's The Big Deal?' Women in the New York City Construction Industry and Sexual Harassment Law, 1970-1985." Cited above as item 220.

378. Becraft, Carolyn H. "Military Women: Policies and Politics." *Bureaucrat*. 20 (Fall 1991): 9-12.

Discusses the recent participation of women in the Persian Gulf War (veterans of that war number at least 35,000 military women), and the fact that combat exclusion has been rendered moot by those events. Outlines recent history of women in the military, and the rise in their representation because of several political and legal decisions in the 1970's. Predicts that the tradition and culture in the armed services, along with the Defense draw-down will perpetuate problems women in the military face. Argues that civilian Political Officials in the Department of Defense as well as Congress must continue to exercise their oversight roles to prevent inequitable treatment of women.

379. Crawford, J.D. "Career Development and Career Choice in Pioneer and Traditional Women." *Journal of Vocational Behavior*. 12 (1987): 129-139.

Notes that women with better-educated mothers are more likely to be "pioneers" (i.e., to choose an "atypical" career profession). Women with less-educated mothers are more likely to choose traditionally female occupations.

380. Duncan, Emily. "Nontraditional Occupations: A Study of Women Who Have Made the Choice." *Vocational Guidance Quarterly*. March, 1985, pp. 241-248.

Provides information on the advantages and disadvantages of a woman's choice to enter a typically male-dominated occupation. Samples 75 women who have chosen nontraditional jobs (skilled craft, labor, and technical fields), and reports on factors that have helped them advance as well as factors that have inhibited their advancement.

381. Ehrhart, Julie Kahn, and Bernice R. Sandler. *Looking For More Than A Few Good Women in Traditionally Male Fields*. Washington: Project on the Status and Education of Women, 1987.

Reports on the under-representation of women in "nontraditional" curricula such as engineering and computer science. Explores reasons for this phenomenon, and recommends courses of action higher education can take to reverse this trend.

382. Falkenberg, L. "The Perceptions of Women Working in Male Dominated Professions." *Canadian Journal of Administrative Sciences*. 5 (June 1988): 77-84.

Attempts to determine if differences in perceptions exist among young, non-supervisory male and female professionals in male dominated professions. Results show that women feel it is assumed that they will have greater problems balancing home and work priorities than men. Women also perceive that they must work harder than men at establishing their status and authority in the workplace.

383. Figart, Deborah M., and Barbara R. Bergmann. *Facilitating Women's Occupational Integration*. Washington: Department of

Labor, Commission on Workforce Quality and Labor Market Efficiency, 1989.

Discusses occupational sex segregation particularly in nontraditionally female jobs. The largest declines in the sex segregation between 1970 and 1980 were in the managerial and professional specialty and service occupations. Examines the relative ease with which laws mandating equal opportunity and affirmative action were as opposed to eliminating institutional and informal obstacles. Examples of these barriers include sexual harassment or co-worker hostility, outmoded administrative rules and procedures by employers and unions, and gender-tracked promotional ladders. Analyzes Federal training programs, and argues that they are doing little to recruit and place women into nontraditional jobs. Cites the Perkins Vocational Education Act as crucial to sustaining the successful community-based pre-apprenticeship training programs that currently exist. Includes sections on sex integration of white-collar work, the impact of technological change on women's work, and policy implications and recommendations.

384. Fisher, Anne B. "Where Women Are Succeeding: They Do Best in Industries Rocked by Change--Computers, Telecommunications, Financial Services--Because Competition Puts a Premium on Sheer Talent." *Fortune.* 116 (August 3, 1987).

Advancement for women is evident in fields like retailing and advertising that traditionally employed women; these fields also held women back, however. Argues that women have better chances of succeeding in fields that are in a constant state of flux. Competition to advance in high technology fields will rely more heavily on pure ability, and will therefore practice less discriminatory employment than traditional fields.

385. Gluck, Sherna Berger. *Rosie the Riveter Revisited: Women, the War, and Social Change.* Bergenfield, NJ: National American Library, 1988.

Through 10 essays of women who worked in the aircraft industry during World War II, details the experiences, barriers, and changes faced by these pioneer women.

386. Goldman, Nancy Loring, ed. *Female Soldiers: Combatants or Noncombatants? Historical and Contemporary Perspectives.* Westport, CT: Greenwood Press, 1982.

A collection of papers on women's experiences in the armed services around the world. Consideration of women serving in combat roles during wartime are discussed in an historical context. Public opinion of women in the military in the United States is examined. Guidelines for effective decision making with regard to women in the military are provided based on the historical and sociological findings.

387. Greene, Pamela. *Nontraditional Occupations for Women: Wages and Prospects for Employment Including an Examination of Self-Supporting Wage Levels.* Oakland, CA: Achievement Council, Inc., 1986.

Using employment data from Rock County, Wisconsin, provides information on the wages of specific traditional and nontraditional occupations. "Traditionally male" and "traditionally female" occupations are identified, and numbers and percents of women in those occupations are given. Also presents mean entry-level and overall wages in Rock County for the occupations examined. Occupations with a predicted favorable future employment outlook are identified using factors like high replacement rate, expected high job growth, and predicted industry expansion. Several tables with narrative explanations of calculations are provided.

*   Heilman, M.E., and J.M. Herlihy. "Affirmative Action, Negative Reaction? Some Moderating Conditions." Cited above as item 137.

*   Heilman, M.E., and R.F. Martell. "Exposure to Successful Women: Antidote to Sex Discrimination in Applicant Screening Decisions?" Cited above as item 206.

*   Heilman, M.E., R.F. Martell, and M.C. Simon. "The Vagaries of Sex Bias: Conditions Regulating the Undervaluation, Equivaluation and Overvaluation of Female Job Applicants." Cited above as item 204.

*   Howell, Ruth S., and Helen Schwartz. "Community-Based Training for Reentry Women in Nontraditional Occupations." Cited above as item 364.

388. Kitfield, James. "Free Force." *Government Executive.* 23 (March 1991): 10-15.

Discusses the effort in the Persian Gulf where for the first time, all-volunteer forces were used. Questions about the disproportionate use of minorities in combat are raised, and issues of women in combat are discussed.

389. ---. "Navy Women: Part of the Team." *All Hands.* No. 855, June 1988: whole issue.

Contents: "Shipmates." "Looking ahead." "Sexual harassment." "DACOWITS." "Making a Difference." "Profiles." "On the Flight Line." "Rights & Benefits."

390. O'Farrell, Brigid., and Sharon L. Harlan. "Craftworkers and

Clerks: The Effect of Male Co-Worker Hostility on Women's Satisfaction with Non-Traditional Jobs." *Social Problems*. 29 (February 1982): 252-265.

Using survey data from female employees in a northeastern company employing over 30,000, finds that women in male-dominated blue-collar jobs are satisfied with their jobs and, contrary to popular belief, women in blue- and white-collar jobs attribute more importance to pay and work content than to positive relationships with co-workers. Discovers, however, a sizable group of blue-collar women who are less satisfied with their work because of harassment from male co-workers. Concludes with an argument that male workers play an important role in perpetuating occupational segregation.

391. Piatz, Brenda. "Women in Non-Traditional Jobs. *Minnesota Cities*. 75 (May 1990): 5-12.

Looks at women employed in municipal public works or public safety units in Minnesota. Includes 3 articles: Women in law enforcement; Fire service; and Public works.

392. Reskin, Barbara F., and Patricia A. Roos. "Job Queues, Gender Queues: Explaining Women's Inroads Into Male Occupations." Philadelphia: Temple University Press, 1990.

Examines changes in the representation of women in traditionally male jobs. Includes 11 case studies of occupations in which women's representation increased at least twice as much during the 1970's as it did in the labor force as a whole.

393. Sanders, Jo Shuchat. *The Nuts and Bolts of Non-Traditional Occupations: How to Help Women Enter Non-Traditional Occupations*. Metuchen, NJ: Scarecrow Press, 1987.

A resource guide for women interested in working in blue-collar trades. Discusses barriers, and gives strategies to overcome barriers. Practical advice is given.

394. Sherwood, Diane. "Women in the Military." *Government Executive.* 21 (August 1989): 10-12, 14-19, 56.

Discusses the representation of women in the military--today, women comprise almost 11 percent of the armed forces. Questions are raised about how these women are doing--economically, psychologically, and socially in the military. A survey is administered to senior women officers; results are given. Includes sections on higher pay, careers for women in the military, the advantages and disadvantages of combat exclusion, sex discrimination and sexual harassment, family issues, and prospects for change.

395. Smith, Emily. "The Women Who Are Scaling High Tech Heights." *Business Week.* (August 28, 1989): 86-88.

Analyzes and discusses factors that have helped women who have made the transition from technical positions to general management.

396. Spencer, A., and D. Podmore. *In a Man's World--Essays on Women in Male-dominated Professions.* London: Tavistock Publications, 1987.

Explores experiences of women in male-dominated fields in Great Britain. Discusses the notion of "discriminatory environments" for women in which their career advancement is stymied because of their gender. Argues that British higher civil service is very homogenous and intolerant of "cultural differences." Also asserts that men and women are assessed differently for promotions and assignments despite standardized performance evaluations. Further asserts that men are assumed competent unless they prove otherwise, while women need to prove their competence. Explores attitudes that affect opportunities for female scientists and refutes myths about pregnancy and natural intellectual ability. Concludes that women must become more aware, male attitudes toward women must change, and the organization of work itself must change before the situation can improve.

397. United States Congress. House. Committee on Armed Services. Military Personnel and Compensation Subcommittee. *Women in the Military.* 101st Cong., 2nd sess. 1990. H.A.S.C. No. 101-63.

An update to a series of three hearings held by the Military Personnel and Compensation Subcommittee 2 years previous to this. Following the first hearing, the Department of Defense, the Navy, and the Marine Corps established task forces on women, which resulted in both openings of additional non-combat positions to women and the strengthening of processes to deal with sexual harassment.

398. United States Congress. Senate. Committee on Labor. *Nontraditional Employment for Women Act: Hearing, June 8, 1989, on S. 975, to Amend the Job Training Partnership Act to Encourage a Broader Range of Training and Job Placement for Women, and For Other Purposes.* 101st Cong., 1st sess., 1989. S. Hearing 101-201.

399. U.S. Department of Labor Women's Bureau. *Directory of Nontraditional Training and Employment Programs Serving Women.* Washington: G.P.O., 1991.

A listing of state-level programs to assist women in obtaining jobs in skilled trades and technical occupations. Provides selected models and services arranged by state.

*   Weiss, Rhoda. "Networking -- Getting Together to Get Ahead." Cited above as item 321.

400. ---. "Women Make Headway in Nontraditional Careers." *National Business Woman*, August/September 1988, pp. 18-23.

Provides statistics showing increased participation by women in selected nontraditional occupations. Profiles several women working in male-dominated occupations, and outlines problems and solutions they have found.

CHAPTER 10

Work & Family Issues

"Equality for women demands a change in the human psyche more profound than anything Marx dreamed of. It means valuing parenthood as much as we value banking." Polly Toynbee

GENERAL ISSUES

401. The Bureau of National Affairs. *Work and Family: A Changing Dynamic.* Washington: Bureau of National Affairs, 1986.

Examines the various policies that are being studied and adopted by both the public and private sectors and unions to meet family demands faced by American workers. Provides information on more than 30 case studies on child care, alternative work schedules, employee assistance programs, and parental leave programs. Also includes information on international trends and labor-management approaches. Questions of responsibility for accommodating family issues in the workplace are discussed.

402. Campbell, Bebe Moore. *Successful Women, Angry Men: Backlash in the Two-Career Marriage.* New York: Random House, 1987.

Outlines issues modern married couples face since the advent of dual-income marriages. Argues that special problems have arisen for these couples as they live with the ideal that men and women are becoming more equal.

403. Clausen, John A., and Martin Gilens. "Personality and Labor Force Participation Across the Life Course: A Longitudinal Study of Women's Careers." *Sociological Forum.* 5 (December 1990): 595-618.

Analyzes the impact of women's labor force experience using data from longitudinal studies of women born between 1920 and 1929. In adolescence, these women were oriented toward marriage and family, yet more than two-thirds eventually spent substantial time employed outside the home. Women who worked more outside the home had more self-confidence, were more status seeking, were more assertive, and invested more in their intellectual development between adolescence and later adulthood.

404. Desai, Sonalde, and Linda J. Waite. *Women's Employment During Pregnancy and After the First Birth: Occupational Characteristics and Work Commitment* (Working Paper No. 26). Population Council, 1991.

Using data from the National Longitudinal Survey of Youth (1979-1986), examines whether female-dominated occupations attract women because they are relatively easy to combine with family responsibilities.

405. Ehrensaft, Diane. *Parenting Together: Men and Women Sharing The Care of Their Children.* New York: The Free Press, 1987.

Details the new relationships that have been forged as a result of economic and social changes. Outlines the psychological and social dynamics of such change related to the family structure and parenting.

406. Ehrlich, E. "The Mommy Track." *Business Week*, March 20, 1989, pp. 126-134.

Discusses problems women face in attempting to balance career pursuits and motherhood. Identifies some new and flexible strategies employed by large corporations in order to keep some of their best women. Examples of such programs include: alternative career paths, extended leaves, flexible scheduling, job sharing and telecommuting. Such practices have led to a phenomenon some have labeled the "mommy track." Some view this phenomenon as positive, while others argue that the "mommy track" is a separate, unequal track that will negatively impact women's careers. Contends that employers must provide both male and female employees with options and support for family life/ work life balance.

407. Farley, Jennie, ed. *The Woman in Management: Career and Family Issues*. Ithaca, N.Y.: Industrial Labor Relations Press. 1983.

Proceedings of a business and professional women's conference sponsored by the Extension and Public Service Division, N.Y. State School of Industrial and Labor Relations, Cornell University, Ithaca, N.Y., in April, 1982.

* Friedman, D.E. "Why the Glass Ceiling?" Cited above as item 93.

408. Goldsmith, Elizabeth B. "In Support of Working Parents and Their Children: Response to Commentary on Scarr et al. Article." *Journal of Social Behavior and Personality*. 5 (November 1990): 517-520.

Examines the importance of fathers to children's development, children's attachment, working vs. nonworking mothers, and quality child care.

409. Hall, Douglas T. "Moving Beyond the 'Mommy Track': An Organization Change Approach." *Personnel.* 66 (December 1989): 23-26.

Discusses controversy caused by Felice Schwartz's article "Management Women and the New Facts of Life." Offers suggestions about how organizations can promote work-family balance by first examining values and assumptions about what "good" executives, parents and careers really are. Focuses on solutions through affirmative corporate and succession planning for advancing women. Argues that companies should focus their change efforts on work-family balance.

410. Jennings, Daniel F. "Special Problems of Married Women at Work." *Baylor Business Review.* 8 (Summer 1990): 9-11.

Argues that child care problems affect the effectiveness of organizations since they can contribute to absenteeism and nonproductive work. Describes a process some career women have begun adopting called "sequencing." These women quit working to rear a family before returning full-time to their careers. Argues that women who do not practice sequencing, face a real dilemma if they want to have children. Delineates several benefits that can be made available for employees who wish to have a family, but do not want to deal with the added stress of working too. Some examples cited include: extended maternity leave with an option to work part-time for a period after the baby's birth, flexible work schedules, job sharing, and working at home.

411. Paulson, Sharon E., Joseph J. Koman, and John P. Hill. "Maternal Employment and Parent-Child Relations in Families of Seventh Graders." (Special Issue: Parent Work and Early Adolescent Development.) *Journal of Early Adolescence* 10 (August 1990): 279-295.

Examines the effects of mothers being employed on closeness between parents and their seventh-grade daughters and sons. One hundred boys and girls were studied. Results showed that in families where the mother is employed, sons report greater closeness with fathers. Daughters report greater closeness with both parents when mothers stay at home or are employed part-time. Employed mothers are closer to sons; and mothers who stay-at-home or are employed part-time report greater closeness to daughters. Fathers reported no differences in closeness to either sons or daughters, regardless of whether the mother was employed.

412. Roos, Patricia A. "Marriage and Women's Occupational Attainment in Cross-Cultural Perspective." *American Sociological Review.* 48 (December 1983): 852-864.

Using data from 12 industrialized countries, examines the differences in the labor market behavior, occupational segregation, and attainment patterns of married and unmarried women. Results support the hypothesis that single women are more similar to men than married women, but not in all aspects of their occupational behavior. Marital responsibilities are shown to affect the extent to which women work and the kinds of jobs in which they are employed. By and large, these differences do not render disparities in career prestige or wage rate. Concludes that women's economic disadvantage cannot be attributed to gender differences in marital responsibilities; also single women do not seem to fare much better than married women as far as career achievement.

413. Schwartz, Felice N. "Management Women and the New Facts of Life." *Harvard Business Review*, January-February 1989, pp. 65-76.

Has become known as the controversial "Mommy Track" article. Identifies two separate groups of women--"career primary" women and "child and family" women. Argues that employing women in management jobs is more expensive than employing men. However, organizations can reduce those costs by being more flexible in order to retain talented women--especially "child and family" women. Argues that while these women are productive and committed, they are not likely to be upwardly mobile for a period of time. However, they are a valuable asset and should be supported in their need for flexibility. Discusses advantages and costs of part-time and shared employment and other family supports (e.g., parental leave for men, support for two-career and single-parent families during relocation, etc.). Good quality child care is identified as the most important element and organizations are encouraged to develop programs.

414. Trenk, Barbara Scherr. "Future Moms, Serious Workers." *Management Review.* 79 (Summer 1990): 33-37.

Discusses the increasing tendency of pregnant women to work up until delivery and return to work soon thereafter. Outlines some programs that exist for pregnant workers.

415. U.S. General Accounting Office. *Comparisons of Federal and Nonfederal Work/Family Programs and Approaches.* Washington: G.A.O, 1992.

After comparing federal work and family programs with several leading nonfederal organizations, concludes that nonfederal organizations are typically more strategic and integrated in their approaches. Further finds that federal programs are not as "family supportive or fully utilized as they could be." Barriers discovered include cost, lack of statutory authority, and concerns that programs are inappropriate for federal employees. Recommendations about the leadership role the U.S. Office of Personnel Management should assume are given.

416. U.S. Office of Personnel Management. *A Study of the Work and Family Needs of the Federal Workforce: A Report to Congress.* Washington: O.P.M., 1992.

Using survey data from the Survey of Federal Employees (SOFE), analyzes work/family needs of federal workers vis-a-vis recruitment, retention, and productivity. Covers such issues as child care, adult dependent care, flexible and compressed work schedules, part-time employment and job sharing, flexiplace, and leave sharing programs. Outlines key measures to increase the effectiveness of work and family programs. Some include: 1) Increasing agency efforts to strengthen their work and family programs; 2) Strengthening OPM's capacity to coordinate policy and provide assistance to agencies; 3) Enhancing interagency cooperation and coordination in developing work and family programs and in resolving related issues; etc.

417. U.S. Office of Personnel Management. *Dependent Care Policies for Federal Employees*. Washington: O.P.M., 1992.

Outlines federal personnel management tools aimed at helping federal employees balance work and family responsibilities, specifically care for children and adult dependents. Covers flexible and compressed work schedules, leave for parental and family responsibilities, leave sharing, part-time employment and job sharing, Employee Assistance Programs, On-site child and adult day care centers, flexiplace, and dependent care referral and information services.

418. Voydanoff, Patricia. "Women, Work, and Family: Bernard's Perspective on the Past, Present, and Future." *Psychology of Women Quarterly*. 12 (September 1988): 269-280.

Analyzes research done by Jessie Bernard on issues of work and family for women. Discusses Bernard's theory of two different worlds of men and women, and raises three major issues related to that theory: problems related to caring, the feminization of work, and family and work roles over the course of a lifetime. Raises several questions and gaps left in Bernard's research about how the separate worlds of men and women can be synthesized and fit into the current and future societal milieu.

CHILD CARE AND OTHER BENEFITS

419. Abraham, Yohannan T., and John S. Bowdidge. "Work-Place Child Care Act: A Prototypical Portrayal of Potential Public Policies." *Public Personnel Management*. 19 (Winter 1990): 411-418.

Argues that a "revolution" is afoot to demand public policy to deal with the employment/childcare crisis. Predicts that by the end of the century, the United States will require employers to provide care for pre-school children of working parents. Sets out a model for such legislation.

420. Cook, Alice H. "Public Policies to Help Dual-Earner Families Meet the Demands of the Work World." *Industrial and Labor Relations Review*. 42 (January 1989): 201-215.

Using examples from several European countries, argues that the United States has been grossly deficient in providing the kind of social and economic support people need to maintain careers and families simultaneously. Argues that we cannot wait for employers to be enlightened enough to provide family-related benefits--we should look at the European models and create the necessary incentives for employers to provide such support.

421. Doherty, Kathleen. "Parental Leave: Strategies for the 1990s." *Business & Health*. 8 (January 1990): 21-23.

Outlines provisions in the Family and Medical Leave Act, which proposed a requirement on employers to give unpaid family leave to parents of newly born, newly adopted, or seriously ill children. Discusses the paucity of family and medical leave policies in organizations, and argues that cost is the primary cause for lack of organizational support. Concludes that employers may be forced to provide such benefits in light of recent political support for parental leave. Innovative companies have begun offering parental leave already, or have given parents an option of working part-time for a period.

422. Friedman, D.E. "The Invisible Barrier to Women in Business." *Across the Board (Inside Guide)*, Winter 1988, pp. 75-79.

Examines the role of the corporation in encouraging a positive future for female *and* male employees by developing strategies, policies, and environments which support family needs. Some of the more innovative efforts by some leading corporations are offered.

423. Hojat, Mohammadreza. "Can Affectional Ties Be Purchased? Comments on Working Mothers and Their Families." *Journal of Social Behavior and Personality.* 5 (November 1990): 493-502.

Argues that Sandra Scarr's proposition that good child care can be purchased in "high-quality" institutions with no bad effects on the children is faulty. Suggests that attachment theory dictates that mothers must be in close proximity, attentive, and responsive to signals in order to instill security in their children. Concludes that working mothers, in general, are less likely than nonworking mothers to satisfy the requirement for secure attachment in their children.

424. LaFleur, Elizabeth K., and Walter B. Newsom. "Opportunities for Child Care." *Personnel Administrator.* 33 (June 1988): 146-149.

Estimates that two-thirds of all children under 6 years will have working mothers by the year 2000. Reports that childcare is the fourth largest expense for working families (after housing, food, and taxes). Argues that companies will be convinced to provide childcare services in order to remain competitive employers. Benefits and problems associated with employer-sponsored childcare programs are discussed.

425. Michelson, William. "Childcare and the Daily Routine. Special Issue: Research on Time Use." *Social Indicators Research*. 23 (December 1990): 353-366.

Shows that women who spend greater amounts of time on outside employment spend less time on other daily responsibilities. Child care helps employed women fulfill home responsibilities, but overall, it does not make daily life easier. Suggests that workplace child care could help decrease some of the tension associated with travel to and from child care facilities.

426. Moss, Peter. "Work, Family and the Care of Children: Issues of Equality and Responsibility." *Children-and-Society*. 4 (Summer 1990): 145-166.

Using examples from Sweden, Spain, and New Zealand, argues that the government should take a leadership role and work with employers, trade unions, local authorities, voluntary organizations, and parents to create viable child-care alternatives for employees and employers. Proposals focus on employment rights for parents, care and education for young children, gender equity, and public funding for policy development.

427. Pulliam, L. Lynne. "Pregnancy Disability and Child Care Leave: What Does VII Require?" *Employee Relations Law Journal*. 17 (Winter 1991/1992): 511-519.

Discusses the provisions of bills before the 102nd Congress on family and child care. Discusses Title VII requirements related to pregnancy disability and child care leave, focusing more comprehensively on the issue of child care. Explains ways employers can develop leave policies that comply with the Pregnancy Discrimination Act without violating Title VII.

428. Scarr, Sandra. "Mother's Proper Place: Children's Needs and Women's Rights." *Journal of Social Behavior and Personality.* 5 (November 1990): 507-515.

Responds to Mohammadreza Hojat's view of problems related to non-maternal care of children of working mothers. Discusses issues of quality of non-maternal child care, effects on children's attachment, and children's emotional, social, and cognitive development.

FLEXIBLE WORK ARRANGEMENTS

429. Buchsbaum, Susan. "Sending 'Care' Packages to the Workplace." *Business & Health.* 9 (May 1991): 56-69.

Cites elder care responsibilities as one of the fastest growing issues with which employees must deal, yet only about 300 companies have policies that assist employees caring for the elderly. Argues that the standard old benefits of health insurance, life insurance, disability, sick days, vacations, and pensions no longer adequately meet the needs of the new working population. Discusses the trend of offering more flexible and innovative benefits to meet these changing needs. Some examples given include: 6-8 weeks maternity leave with pay, extended leave without pay, paternity leave, family sick days, dependent care days, flexible time, dependent care referral services, get-well rooms for mildly ill children, and back-up child care.

430. Calise, Angela K. "Parents Push for Time Off After Childbirth." *National Underwriter.* 94 (July 16, 1990): 4,14.

Outlines the recent debate over the right of parents to stay home with their newborn child for a transition period without fear of losing their jobs and health insurance coverage. Cites a recent ruling by the 3rd Circuit U.S. Court of Appeals which holds that men should be entitled to unpaid child-rearing leave if that benefit is offered to women. The decision is binding in three states.

431. Connors, Nancy. "Job Sharing: Beyond Maternity Leave." *CFO: The Magazine for Chief Financial Officers*. 6 (March 1990): 47-49.

Citing research from the firm Catalyst on flexible work arrangements among professional and managerial employees at 50 large firms, finds that about 1/3 of the firms surveyed have job-sharing programs. Of the employees in the study who have with flexible work arrangements, 85% are women with young children. Issues of communication between management and job sharers, between other staff and job sharers, and between the job sharers themselves are deemed crucial to the success of such programs. Cautions that a job-sharing program is a helpful program for many employees, but it should not be thought of as a panacea. Argues that problems related to child care and elder care will continue whether employees work part-time or full-time.

432. Cooley, Cathy A. "1989 Employee Benefits Address Family Concerns." *Monthly Labor Review*. 113 (June 1990): 60-63.

Outlines the Bureau of Labor Statistic's 1989 findings from their Employee Benefits Survey, which presents information on the incidence and characteristics of employee benefits available to full-time workers in private sector establishments employing 100 or more workers. Findings include: 1. Paid maternity leave is available to nearly two-fifths of employees, and unpaid paternity leave is available to almost one-fifth of workers. 2. Flexible work arrangements were provided to one-tenth of employees.

433. Federally Employed Women. *Survey of Flexible Work Arrangements*. Washington: Federally Employed Women, Inc., 1992.

Outlines the types of flexible work arrangements available to employees in the federal sector, including flexitime, maxiflex or compressed work schedules, part-time employment, and job-sharing. Using survey data on the availability of flexible work arrangements, finds that although these options exist in the federal system, 60% of respondents do not feel they have adequate access to them. Concludes that although the federal government is far ahead of state and local governments and the private sector when it comes to flexible workplace policies, there is great room for improvement. Recommends 1) further education of management officials to encourage support for these programs, 2) further recognition and support of employees who are juggling work and family responsibilities, 3) developing a formal family and medical leave policy, and 4) expanding access to child care services.

434. Field, Susan, and Lorraine Paddison. "Designing a Career Break System." *Industrial & Commercial Training* (UK). 21 (January/February 1989): 22-25.

Discusses the recent trend of employers offering "career breaks" in Great Britain. Such programs allow both women and men to take a hiatus from employment while their children are pre-school age. Employees are then encouraged to return to the same employer on previous terms and conditions. Argues that this policy has been especially helpful given changes to the workforce, including increasing skill shortages and the decrease in the numbers of young recruits for employment. Guidelines and examples for designing such a program are given.

435. Harris, Diane. "Maternity Leave--Yours: Maternity Leave--Hers." *Working Woman*. 16 (August 1991): 56-59, 86-87.

Cites statistics which estimate that 70% to 80% of all women currently in the labor force are of child-bearing age, and between 80% and 90% of them are likely to become pregnant during the course of their careers. Unfortunately, employer responses to these statistics have been relatively slow. Gives four issues to consider when they are looking at maternity leave: 1. manager's reaction, 2. negotiation of leave details, 3. management of the leave, and 4. gradual easing back into the job upon return. Argues that compromise is key in the negotiation process. Cites a study which shows that 78% of women who work for organizations which actively accommodate their needs return to their jobs after childbirth.

436. Herchenroether, Sherry. "Family Leave, Without Labor Pains." *Working Woman.* 17 (January 1992): 27,30.

Outlines the maternity leave program implemented at Aetna Life & Casualty which developed because the original policy which gave employees 6 weeks of paid disability, resulted in the best employees not returning to work. In 1988, Aetna designed a family-leave program that gave employees up to 6 months off, without pay, for births, adoptions, or serious illness in the family in addition to the original 6 weeks of disability. Other flexible benefits like part-time work or working out of the home were also offered as an option to some employees. Results of the new program were very positive--88% of the new mothers who had taken time off were retained in the first year, and the amount of family leave time employees actually took tended to be shorter than what was originally anticipated.

437. Joice, Wendell H. "Home Based Employment: A Consideration for Public Personnel Management." *Public Personnel Management.* 20 (Spring 1991): 49-60.

Discusses the U.S. Office of Personnel Management's home based employment (HBE) pilot initiative. Covers background and characteristics of the program, and makes recommendations about HBE programs to meet future workforce needs, including family responsibilities.

438. Orr, Elaine L. "Policies for the Family-Friendly Workplace." *Bureaucrat.* 20 (Fall 1991): 5-8.

Outlines policies that employers should consider to deal with the predicted changing demographics, and increased personal demands on employees. Gives examples of several benefits related to health care, child care, elder care from private industry and government. Argues employers who provide such benefits will have employees who experience less stress, and can therefore be more productive. Concludes by outlining the provisions of the "Family Leave Act."

439. Ralson, David A. "How Flexitime Eases Work/Family Tensions." *Personnel.* 67 (August 1990): 45-48.

Analyzes results from a survey of 115 women who recently changed to flexitime schedules. Results show that women find it easier to coordinate their off-job and on-job responsibilities, absenteeism decreases, and level of performance is improved. Concludes also that flexitime can help reduce interrole conflict which often contributes to women's absenteeism.

440. U.S. Merit Systems Protection Board. *Balancing Work Responsibilities and Family Needs: The Federal Civil Service Response.* Washington: G.P.O., 1991.

Report evaluating the flexible work arrangements offered by the federal government. Argues that federal managers must create work environments that are not only not hostile to work and family concerns, but are proactive in their support of such concerns. Further supports the notion that flexible work arrangements improve the morale of employees, increases their productivity, and lowers turnover rates--ultimately saving the federal government money.

441. Verespej, Michael A. "Family Leave? It's Here." *Industry Week.* 240 (March 4, 1991): 30.

Cites 8 states plus the District of Columbia which have passed family-leave bills, and outlines their common features. These include: either parent can take the leave; leave can be used for adoptions; employers must make health insurance coverage available to employees while on leave; and job protection is provided. The State family-leave laws do differ on what size a company must be to comply and how long a leave employers must provide. Argues that this trend will continue unless a Federal law is passed which preempts it.

442. ---. "Europe Today May Foreshadow U.S. Benefits." *Employee Benefit Plan Review.* 45 (September 1990): 38-39.

Forecasts changes in benefits in the United States, arguing that we tend to lag behind countries who first adopt particular social welfare policies by about 30 years. Argues that the regular workweek is likely to decrease to 32-34 hours by 2000, following Norway's lead where the average workweek already stands at 25.6 hours. One motivator of increased time off is the need to care for children or other family members. Sweden mandates up to 12 months of paid maternity leave.

443. ---. "Giving Employees Time, Flexibility." *Employee Benefit Plan Review.* 44 (May 1990): 16-18.

Such work policies as flexible schedules, flexible workplace, job sharing, and family care leave are becoming popular methods for assisting employees with family concerns. Flexible schedules to accommodate dependent care is a valuable employee benefit that often does not involve additional expense. With job sharing, 2 employees share responsibility for one full-time position. As of the end of 1988, New York state agencies had 7,000 salaried employees working part-time. A flexible workplace allows an employee to work at home instead of at the office. A 1988 survey estimated that there were 25 million home-based workers, and it has predicted that there will be 40 million such workers by the year 2000. According to a Bureau of National Affairs survey, 75% of employers offer parental leave. However, a Bureau of Labor Statistics survey indicated that only 2% of female employees had paid maternity leave.

444. ---. "Working Around Motherhood: As Women Move Up the Ladder, Companies Offer Part-Time Hours, 'Flexitime,' Child Care." *Business Week*. May 24, 1982.

Examines flexible policies being used by companies to help women professionals deal with child care issues.

445. ---. "Working At a Distance." *Worklife Report* (Canada). 8 (No. 2, 1991): 8-9.

Discusses a new trend in the workplace that has resulted from improved information and communication technologies--telework. Telework is a flexible work arrangement which allows employees to work in a site other than the traditional workplace (e.g., customer sites, satellite centers, at home). Reports on an International Labour Organization study show that telework can lead to productivity gains of up to 60%. Argues that telework allows workers who would otherwise be forced to leave, such as women after maternity leave and senior workers nearing retirement, to stay. Cites improvement of time flexibility and greater autonomy as benefits to employees. Disadvantages include: lower pay, reduced benefits, isolation, and exploitation. But concludes that combining telework with time spent in the traditional work site can help to mitigate the disadvantages.

MULTIPLE ROLES & COMPETING DEMANDS

446. Akabas, Sheila H. "Women, Work and Mental Health: Room for Improvement." Special Issue: Prevention Strategies in the Problems of Women. *Journal of Primary Prevention.* 9 (Fall/Winter 1988): 130-140.

Analyzes physical and mental health problems resulting from multiple roles that women play in today's society. Suggests that working conditions, increased use of computers, and lower-paid jobs contribute to the excessive stress that some women face--thus affecting their physical and mental well-being. Advocates for preventive measures to help women such as better childcare and eldercare services, better working conditions and higher-paying jobs, and working to make family responsibilities more shared between the sexes.

447. Biernat, Monica, and Camille B. Wortman. *Journal of Personality and Social Psychology.* 60 (June 1991): 844-860.

Analyzes a sample of 139 professional couples with young children. Concludes that the traditional inequities in the allocation of child-care tasks and home responsibility still exist. Overall, women were more self-critical than were men about their performance in home roles, and women professionals continue to use traditional sex-role standards to evaluate their "performance." Discusses the need to allow for both partners' perspective vis-a-vis home responsibilities.

448. Beutell, Nicholas J., and Marianne M. O'Hare. "Work-Nonwork Conflict Among MBAs: Sex Differences in Role Stressors and Life Satisfaction. *Work and Stress.* 1 (January-March 1987): 35-41.

Analyzes work-nonwork conflict among 271 part-time graduate students by investigating work-role conflict, career salience, age, length of tenure, and number of children living at home. Also examines the relationship between work-nonwork conflict and "life satisfaction." Concludes that there are no differences between men and women related to work-nonwork conflict; and work-role conflict is most closely related to work-nonwork conflict for both sexes. Also concludes that "life satisfaction" is highly related to work-nonwork conflict, except for single women.

449. Davidson, Marilyn, and Cary Cooper. "Women Managers: Work, Stress and Marriage." *International Journal of Social Economics.* 12:(No. 2, 1985): 17-25.

Examines several issues married women executives in Great Britain face. Discusses stress stemming from pressures of both work and home environments and responsibilities, and the differences between the way men and women handle stress.

450. Hall, Holly. "A Woman's Place ...." *Psychology Today.* 22 (April 1988): 28-29.

Asserts that even though women juggle many and varied responsibilities when they choose to work, they are reaping many benefits as well. Suggests that women who are satisfied with their jobs are less depressed and anxious than stay-at-home women, and women who work are much more likely to feel fulfilled.

451. Haw, Mary A. "Women, Work and Stress: A Review and Agenda for the Future." *Journal of Health and Social Behavior.* 23 (June 1982): 132-144.

Reviews the literature on women and work-related stress. Stress is defined as "an imbalance between perceived demand and perceived capability." Argues that work may have a beneficial impact on mental well-being, but that certain types of jobs, when combined with family responsibilities may lead to increased risk of cardiovascular disease. Unfortunately, studies on women lack specificity in work environments, family responsibilities, and attitudes. Expresses the need for future research in this area.

452. Hemmelgarn, Brenda, and Gail Laing. "The Relationship Between Situational Factors and Perceived Role Strain in Employed Mothers." *Family and Community Health.* 14 (April 1991): 8-15.

Examines stress experienced by women returning to work after the birth of their first child. Concludes that the confidence and comfort a woman experiences in the maternal role is strongly related to role strain. High maternal identity related to lower role strain, and women who were satisfied with their current job experienced less role strain.

453. McBride, Angela B. "The Challenges of Multiple Roles: The Interface Between Work and Family When Children Are Young." *Prevention in Human Services.* 9 (No. 1, 1990): 143-156.

Provides guidance on stress management and avoidance, stress resistance building, and stress reaction management as strategies for dealing with multiple demands. Outlines available quality child care, parental leave, and other options for minimizing stress. Discusses issues related to sharing home responsibilities between professionally employed women and their husbands.

454. Miller, Angela B. "Earning Bread and Baking Bread: Reconciling Worklife and Familylife." *Employee Assistance Quarterly* 5 (No. 4, 1990): 83-88.

Discusses the various sources of stress experienced by parents who work, including: how well they split their time between family and work, finding good child care, conflict between the competing expectations as parents and as employees, and an overload of obligations. Suggests that employee assistance programs (EAPS) can help employees meet the demands of parenting and working by helping them develop life management skills and by providing child care information and referral services.

455. Nelson, Debra L., James C. Quick, Michael A. Hitt, and Doug Moesel. "Politics, Lack of Career Progress, and Work/Home Conflict: Stress and Strain for Working Women." *Sex Roles.* 23 (August 1990): 169-185.

Examines stress experienced by 195 professional women in terms of politics, lack of career progress, and work/home conflicts. Shows that politics and lack of career progress are related to greater stress and reduced satisfaction. Work/home conflicts seems to be associated with greater stress, but are unrelated to satisfaction.

456. Schneider, Barbara Ann, and Deborah Conway. "Married Women, Employment Status, and Stress: A Critical Review and Agenda for the Future," Research paper, Biola University (California), 1987.

Reviews research in comparisons of employed women and unemployed women related to depression, psychological problems, alienation, role conflict, marital problems, personal satisfaction, job satisfaction, and anxiety. Concludes from this review that there are no differences between employed and unemployed women vis-a-vis these issues. Those studies which do report differences tend to show that employed women experienced less psychological stress than unemployed women.

457. Shukla, Archana, and Nidhi Shukra. "Work and Wellbeing: Significance of Marital Status and Education." *Journal of the Indian Academy of Applied Psychology.* 12 (July 1986): 59-63.

Study of 116 women (62 employed and 54 unemployed) to discover the relationship between employment and "psychological well-being." Also evaluated the effects of marital status and education as moderators. Results show that employed women are as happy as unemployed women; there is a greater difference between the psychological well-being of single women (employed vs. unemployed) and married women; and highly educated women seem happier when they are employed, especially if they are single.

458. Walker, Lorraine O., and Mary A. Best. "Well-Being of Mothers with Infant Children: A Preliminary Comparison of Employed Women and Homemakers." *Women and Health.* 17 (No. 1, 1991): 71-89.

Compares stress levels and lifestyles in mothers who are homemakers and mothers employed full-time outside the home. Employed mothers reported greater perceived stress in their lives and less healthy lifestyles compared to homemakers. The most frequently reported sources of stress for employed mothers were conflicts or problems about returning to work, lack of time, fatigue and sleep disturbance, work overload, and illness of children. Concludes that employed mothers may neglect themselves to cope with work overload resulting in relatively worse personal health.

459. Weaver, Charles N., and Michael D. Matthews. "Work Satisfaction of Females with Full-Time Employment and Full-Time Housekeeping: 15 Years Later." *Psychological Reports.* 66 (June 1990): 1248-1250.

Using perceptual data, it is argued that women who work full-time outside the home have greater work satisfaction than women engaged in full-time housework.

460. Witt, L. Alan, and John W. Wilson. "Breadwinning Status as a Moderator of the Equity-Job Satisfaction Relationship." *Psychological Reports*. 66 (June 1990): 1361-1362.

Analyzes questionnaire results from 44 married female schoolteachers and 26 married female workers in a military organization. Results show that perceptions of equity were stronger predictors of job satisfaction for those women who were the family breadwinners than for those whose husbands worked (i.e., the nonbreadwinners).

461. Wong, Lisa M. L. "Working Women." *Public Personnel Management*, 17 (Spring 1988): 29-39.

Discusses the various and competing roles women are playing in today's society, as well as the effects on their lifestyles as they learn to juggle work, home, and children. Argues that as women's roles continue to change, so do their attitudes and strategies for coping with multiple demands.

RESOURCES

General

1) Bank Street College of Education, 610 West 112th Street, New York, NY 10025, (212) 663-7200.

2) Bureau of National Affairs, Inc., 1231 25th Street, NW., Washington, DC 20037, (202) 452-4200.

3) Catalyst, 250 Park Avenue South, New York, NY 10002, (212) 777-8900.

4) Coalition of Labor Union Women, 15 Union Square, New York, NY 10003, (212) 242-0700.

5) The Conference Board, Work and Family Information Center, 845 Third Avenue, New York, NY 10022, (212) 759-0900.

6) Families and Work Institute, c/o Dana Friedman and Ellen Galinsky, 110 Summit Road, Port Washington, NY 11050.

7) Family Resource Coalition, Suite 1625, 230 North Michigan Avenue, Chicago, IL 60601, (312) 726-4750.

8) Family Services America, 11700 West Lake Park Drive, Park Place, Milwaukee, WI 53224, (414) 359-2111.

9) National Federation of Independent Business, 600 Maryland Avenue, SW., Washington, DC 20024, (202) 554-9000.

10) 9 to 5, National Association of Working Women, 614 Superior Avenue, NW., Cleveland, OH 44113, (216) 566-9308.

11) Service Employees International Union, AFL-CIO, 1313 L Street, NW., Washington, DC 20005, (202) 898-3200.

12) U.S. Department of Health and Human Services, 200 Independence Avenue, SW., Washington, DC 20201, (202) 245-6296.

13) U.S. Department of Labor, Bureau of Labor Statistics, 441 G Street, NW., Washington, DC 20212, (202) 523-1222.

14) U.S. Department of Labor, Women's Bureau, 200 Constitution Avenue, NW., Washington, DC 20210, (202) 523-6652.

15) U.S. Small Business Administration, 1441 L Street, NW., Washington, DC 20416, (202) 653-6554.

16) Wellesley College Center for Research on Women, Wellesley College, Wellesley, MA 02181, (617) 431-1453.

17) Women's Bureau, U.S. Department of Labor, Clearinghouse on Work and Family, 200 Constitution Avenue, NW., Washington, DC 20210, (202) 523-4486.

Benefits

1) Employee Benefit Research Institute, 2121 K Street, NW., Suite 1600, Washington, DC 20037, (202) 775-6356.

2) Employers Council on Flexible Compensation, 1660 L Street, NW., Washington, DC 20036, (202) 659-4300.

3) National Women's Law Center, 1616 P Street, NW., Suite 100, Washington, DC 20036, (202) 328-5160.

Leave Policies

1) Association of Junior Leagues, 660 First Avenue, New York, NY 10016, (212) 683-1515.

2) Congressional Caucus on Women's Issues, 2471 Rayburn House Office Building, Washington, DC 20515, (202) 226-6740.

3) International Foundation on Employee Benefit Plans, 18700 West Bluemound Road, P.O. Box 69, Brookfield, WI 53005, (414) 786-6700.

4) National Center for Clinical Infant Programs, 733 15th Street, NW., Washington, DC 20005, (202) 347-0308.

5) National Council of Jewish Women, 53 West 23rd Street, 6th Floor, New York, NY 10010, (212) 645-4048.

6) NOW Legal Defense Fund, 99 Hudson Street, 12th Floor, New York, NY 10013, (212) 925-6635.

7) Yale Bush Center in Child Development and Social Policy, Yale University, P.O. Box 11A, Yale Station, New Haven, CT 06520-7447, (203) 432-4577.

Alternative Work Schedules

1) Association of Part-Time Professionals, The Flow General Building, 7655 Old Springhouse Road, McLean, VA 22102, (703) 734-7975.

2) Gil Gordon Associates, 10 Donner Court, Monmouth Junction, NJ 08852, (201) 329-2266.

3) New Ways to Work, 149 Ninth Street, San Francisco, CA 94103, (415) 555-1000.

4) Project for Home Based Work, c/o Kathleen Christensen, Center for Human Environments, The Graduate School and University Center of the City University of New York, 33 West 42nd Street, New York, NY 10036, (212) 642-2530.

5) Work in America Institute of Scarsdale, 700 White Plains Road, Scarsdale, NY 10583, (914) 472-9600.

Child Care

1) Center for Parenting Studies, Wheelock College, 200 The Riverway, Boston, MA 02215, (617) 734-5200, ext. 150.

2) Child Care Action Campaign, 99 Hudson Street, Room 1233, New York, NY 10013, (212) 334-9595.

3) Child Care Law Center, 22 Second Street, San Francisco, CA 94105, (415) 495-5498.

4) Children's Defense Fund, 122 C Street, NW., Washington, DC 20001, (202) 628-8787.

5) Home and School Institute, Inc., 1201 16th Street, NW., Room 228, Washington, DC 20036, (202) 466-3633.

6) National Association for the Education of Young Children, 1834 Connecticut Avenue, NW., Washington, DC 20009, (800) 424-2460.

7) National Association of Hospital Affiliated Child Care Programs, c/o Documensions, 11 North Batavia Avenue, Batavia, IL 60510, (312) 879-0050.

8) Regional Research Institute for Human Services, Portland State University, P.O. Box 751, Portland, OR 97207-0751, (503) 229-4040.

9) School-Age Child Care Project, Wellesley College Center for Research on Women, Wellesley, MA 02181, (617) 235-0320.

Elder Care

1) American Association of Retired Persons, 1909 K Street, NW., Washington, DC 20049, (202) 872-4700.

2) American Society on Aging, 833 Market Street, Suite 516, San Francisco, CA 94103, (415) 543-2617.

3) Center for the Study of Aging, University of Bridgeport, 170 Lafayette Street, Bridgeport, CT 06601, (203) 576-4358.

4) National Council on Aging, 600 Maryland Avenue, SW., Washington, DC 20024, (202) 479-1200.

5) New York Business Group on Health, 622 Third Avenue, 34th Floor, New York, NY 10017, (212) 808-0550.

6) Older Women's League, 730 11th Street, NW., 3rd Floor, Washington, DC 20001, (202) 783-6686.

7) Philadelphia Geriatrics Center, 5301 Old York Road, Philadelphia, PA 19141, (215) 456-2900.

8) Regional Research Institute for Human Services, Portland State University, P.O. Box 751, Portland, OR 97207-0751, (503) 229-4040.

9) Washington Business Group on Health, Institute on Aging, Work and Health, 229 1/2 Pennsylvania Avenue, SE., Washington, DC 20003, (202) 547-6644.

Relevant Publications by the Women's Bureau, U.S. Department of Labor

Fact Sheets:

1) State Maternity/Paternal Leave Laws. 90-1. 1990. 8 p.

2) Working Mothers and Their Children. 89-3. 1989. 8 p.
3) Women Who Maintain Families. (In press).
4) Alternative Work Patterns. 86-3. 1986. 4 p.
5) Caring for Elderly Family Members. 86-4. 1986. 4 p.

Other:

Work and Family Resource Kit. 1989. 20 p.

The Pregnancy Discrimination Act

(From the U.S. Office of Personnel Managements's Fact Sheet on *The Pregnancy Discrimination Act*).

The Pregnancy Discrimination Act is an amendment to Title VII of the Civil Rights Act of 1964 which prohibits among other things, discrimination in employment on the basis of sex. The Act makes it clear that discrimination on the basis of pregnancy, childbirth or related medical conditions constitutes unlawful sex discrimination under Title VII.

The basic principle of the Act is that women affected by pregnancy and related conditions must be treated the same as other applicants and employees on the basis of their ability or inability to work.

The Equal Employment Opportunity Commission has issued guidelines including questions and answers, interpreting the Act. These guidelines provide guidance as to what employment practices would be considered by the Commission as violating the Act.

Hiring
The guidelines provide that an employer cannot refuse to hire a woman because of her pregnancy-related condition so long as she is able to perform the major functions necessary to the job. Further, an employer

cannot refuse to hire her because of its prejudices against pregnant workers or the prejudices of co-workers, clients, or customers.

Health Insurance

Any health insurance provided by an employer must cover expenses for pregnancy-related conditions on the same basis as expenses for other medical conditions. However, health insurance for expenses arising from abortion is not required except where life of the mother would be endangered if the fetus were carried to term, or where medical complications have arisen from an abortion.

Pregnancy-related expenses should be reimbursed in the same manner as are expenses incurred for other medical conditions. Therefore, whether a plan reimburses the employees on a fixed basis, or a percentage of reasonable and customary charge basis, the same basis should be used for reimbursement of expenses incurred for pregnancy-related conditions.

The amounts payable for the costs incurred for pregnancy-related conditions can be limited only to the same extent as are costs for other conditions. Neither an additional deductible, an increase in the usual deductible, nor a larger deductible can be imposed for coverage of pregnancy-related medical costs, whether as a condition for inclusion of pregnancy-related costs in the policy or for payment of the costs when incurred. Thus, if pregnancy-related costs are the first incurred under the policy, the employee is required to pay only the same deductible as would otherwise be required had other medical costs been the first incurred. Once this deductible has been paid, no additional deductible can be required for other medical procedures.

If a health insurance plan excludes the payment of benefits for any conditions existing at the time the insured's coverage becomes effective (pre-existing condition clause), benefits can be denied for medical costs arising from a pregnancy existing at the time the coverage became effective.

Pregnancy and Maternity Leave

An employer may not single out pregnancy-related conditions for special procedures for determining an employee's ability to work. However, an employer may use any procedure used to determine the ability of all employees to work. For example, if an employer requires its employees to submit a doctor's statement concerning their inability to work before granting leave or paying sick benefits, the employer may require employees affected by pregnancy-related conditions to submit such statements.

An employer is required to treat an employee temporarily unable to perform the functions of her job because of her pregnancy-related condition in the same manner as it treats other temporarily disabled employees, whether by providing modified tasks, alternative assignments, disability leaves, leaves without pay, etc.

An employee must be permitted to work at all times during pregnancy when she is able to perform her job. If an employee has been absent from work as a result of a pregnancy-related condition and recovers, her employer may not require her to remain on leave until after her baby is born. Further, an employer may not have a rule which prohibits an employee from returning to work for a predetermined length of time after childbirth.

Fringe Benefits
An employer may not limit benefits for pregnancy-related conditions to married employees. Further, if an employer has an all-female work force or job classification, the employer must provide benefits for pregnancy-related conditions if benefits are provided for other conditions.

If an employer provides benefits to employees on leave, such as installment purchase disability insurance, payment of premiums for health, life or other insurance, continued payments into pension, saving or profit-sharing plans, the employer must provide the same benefits for those on leave for pregnancy-related conditions.

Again, the principle that pregnancy-related disabilities should be treated the same as other temporary disabilities applies to the accrual and crediting of seniority, to the calculation of vacation and pay increases, and to benefits for temporary disabilities.

Right to Return to Work
Unless the employee on leave for pregnancy-related conditions has informed the employer that she does not intend to return to work, her job must be held open for her return on the same basis as jobs are held open for employees on sick or disability leave for other reasons.

Child Care
While leave for child care purposes is not covered by the Pregnancy Discrimination Act, Title VII principles would require that leave for child care purposes be granted on the same basis as leave which is granted to employees for other non-medical reasons. For example, if an employer allows its employees to take leave without pay or accrued annual leave for travel or education which is not job related, the same type of leave must be granted to those who wish to remain on leave for infant care, even though they are medically able to work.

For Further Details, Consult 29 CFR PART 1604

CHAPTER 11

Bibliographies & Other General Resources

"For this, indeed, is the true source of our ignorance--the fact that our knowledge can only be finite, while our ignorance must necessarily be infinite." Sir Karl Popper.

PERTINENT BIBLIOGRAPHIES

462. Ballou, Patricia K. *Women: A Bibliography of Bibliographies.* New York: Macmillan. 1986.

An annotated bibliography of bibliographies covering 1970-1985. Subjects covered include history, literature, religion, economics, employment, occupations, psychology and health.

463. Davis, Mari. *Work and Family Functioning: An Annotated Bibliography Selected from Family Database.* Melbourne, Australia: Australian Institute of Family Studies, Family Information Centre, 1987.

An annotated bibliography which lists works published in Australia on issues related to work and family responsibilities. Some topics covered include: career development and effects on family life; discrimination and employment; child care, work, and family; economics, family life, and employment; one parent families and employment; stress at work and family life technological change and employment; the value of work and attitudes to employment; working mothers and family functioning women, employment issues, and family life.

464. Dixon, Penelope. *Mothers and Mothering: An Annotated Bibliography.* New York: Garland Publishing, Inc., 1991.

Includes 351 entries. Gives the feminist perspective on mothering in today's world. Sections on working mothers, single mothers, mothering today, and mothering and the family are included.

465. Gibish, Jane E. *Women in the Armed Forces: Special Bibliographic Series* (No. 228), Maxwell Air Force Base, Alabama: Air University Library, 1986.

466. Hurst, Marsha, and Ruth Zambrana. *Determinants and Consequences of Maternal Employment: An Annotated Bibliography, 1976-1980.* Washington: Business and Professional Women's Foundation, 1981.

198 entries of professional articles and academic studies as well as "popular" literature and books on child care and employment issues for women.

467. Jacobs, Daniel J., "Sexual Harassment and Related Issues: A Selective Bibliography." *Record of the Association of the Bar of the City of New York.* 46 (December 1991): 930-938.

Selected bibliography of works on sexual harassment.

468. Jorgensen, Mary Anne. *A Directory of Selected Research & Policy Centers Working on Women's Issues.* Washington: Women's Research. 1989.

Lists a wide variety of centers which concentrate on women's studies issues, including employment and social policy issues.

469. Kennedy, Susan Estabrook. *America's White Working-Class Women: A Historical Bibliography*. New York: Garland Publishing, Inc., 1981.

470. Leavitt, Judith A. *American Women Managers and Administrators: A Selective Bibliographical Dictionary of 20th Century Leaders in Business, Education, and Government*. Westport, CT: Greenwood Press, 1985.

Provides biographies of 226 American women managers and leaders. Also includes bibliographies by and about the women included.

471. Leavitt, Judith A. *Women in Administration and Management: An Information Sourcebook*. Phoenix: Oryx Press, 1988.

Over 900 entries including articles in "popular" as well as academic journals. Covers such topics as progress and status of women in management; sex-role stereotypes; and obstacles to advancement. Also lists "classics" that the author thinks should be part of any core library. Pertinent associations and directories are also listed.

472. Leavitt, Judith A. *Women in Management: An Annotated Bibliography and Sourcelist*. Phoenix: Oryx Press, 1982.

Updated edition of *Women in Management, 1970-1979*.

473. McCaghy, M. Dawn. *Sexual Harassment; A Guide to Resources*. Boston: G.K. Hall and Company, 1985.

Covers general works as well as coping strategies, legal issues, and management response to sexual harassment in the workplace. Period of concentration is 1974-1984.

474. McCullough, Rita J., ed. *Sources: An Annotated Bibliography of Women's Issues.* Manchester, Connecticut: Knowledge, Ideas & Trends, Inc., 1991.

Comprehensive coverage of a variety of women's issues. Some topics include health, labor, history of women, as well as humor, education, and women and men.

475. McFeely, Mary Drake, ed. *The Women's Annual, 1984-1985.* New York: Macmillan, 1985.

Includes essays on women in science, women in nontraditional occupations, and health issues of the aging.

476. National Council for Research on Women. *A Women's Mailing List Directory.* Washington: National Council for Research on Women, 1990.

Descriptions of lists maintained by a variety of American women's groups and organizations; includes size, format, and sharing policies. Groups listed include research centers and caucuses, feminist periodicals, publishers, bookstores, and women's policy and activist organizations.

477. Watkins, Kathleen Pullan, and Lucius Durant, Jr. *Day Care: A Source Book.* New York: Garland Publishing, 1989.

Emphasizes standards in the field, issues and innovations in the Day Care industry.

478. Wilkinson, Carroll Wetzel. *Women Working in Nontraditional Fields: References and Resources 1963-1988*. Boston: G.K. Hall & Company, 1991.

Includes articles and books on women in the Trades (construction, carpentry, fire fighting, etc.); the Professions (engineers, scientists, surgeons, etc.); and high-technology professions. Introduction covers historical background and current findings related to women in nontraditional careers.

479. Wilson, Guy, and Charlotte Hurley. *Women in the Workplace: The 1980's and Beyond*. Washington: G.A.O., 1985.

Covers literature in several areas including discrimination, pay disparities, benefits, retirement, health and safety, and management. Gives few annotations; intended to provide sources to researchers.

GENERAL RESOURCES

Publications of the Women's Bureau, U.S. Department of Labor

<u>Women in the Work Force</u>

Fact Sheets:
1) Women Workers: Outlook to 2005. 92-1. 1992. 8 p.
2) Women With Work Disabilities. 92-1. 1992. 8 p.
3) 20 Facts on Women Workers. 90-2. 1990. 4 p.
4) Earnings Differences Between Women and Men. 90-3. 8 p.
5) Black Women in the Labor Force. 90-4. 1990. 4 p.
6) Women in the Skilled Trades and Other Manual Occupations. 90-5. 1990. 8 p.
7) Women of Hispanic Origin in the Labor Force. 89-1. 1989. 4 p.
8) La Mujer de Origen Hispano en la Fuerza Laboral. 89-1s. 1989. 4 p.
9) Women in Labor Organizations. 89-2. 1989. 4 p.
10) Women in Management. 89-4. 1989. 8 p.
11) Women Business Owners. 89-6. 1989. 2 p.
12) Hispanic Origin Women Business Owners. 89-8. 1989. 2 p.
13) Black Women Business Owners. 89-7. 1989. 3p.
14) Asian American Women Business Owners. 89-8. 1989. 2 p.
15) American Indian/Alaska Native Women Business Owners. 89-9. 1989. 2 p.

Booklets:
1) A Working Woman's Guide To Her Job Rights. (In Press).
2) Directory of Nontraditional Training and Employment Programs Serving Women. 1991.
3) Employers and Child Care: Benefiting Work and Family. Reprinted 1990.
4) Women on the Job: Careers in the Electronic Media. 1990.
5) Flexible Workstyles: A Look at Contingent Labor. 1988.
6) Jobs for the Future. Reprinted 1988.

7) Employment-Focused Programs for Adolescent Mothers. Reprinted 1987.

Research Organizations

Center for Women Policy Studies
2000 P Street, NW
Suite 508
Washington, DC 20036
(202) 872-1770
Leslie R. Wolfe, Executive Director

Research Activities: Policy issues affecting legal, social, educational, and economic status of women. Projects focus on education for women and girls of color, women and AIDS, violence against women, sexual harassment in the workplace, reproductive laws for the 1990's, work and family issues, and occupational segregation and its roots in education. Designs model legislation and develops and disseminates program models.

Columbia University, Institute for Research on Women and Gender
763 Schermerhorn Extension
New York, NY 10027
(212) 854-3277
Martha Howell, Director

Research Activities: Women as related to race and class.

Cornell University, Institute for Women and Work
15 East 26th Street
New York, NY 10010
(212) 340-2825
Anne H. Nelson, Director

Research Activities: Conducts applied research with a view to develop, test, and provide educational programs that help working women fulfill their educational and career goals and participate more effectively in the organizations to which they belong.

Institute for Women's Policy Research
1400 20th Street, NW
Suite 104
Washington, DC 20036
(202) 785-5100
Heidi I. Hartmann, Ph.D., Director

Research Activities: Causes and consequences of women's poverty, particularly of minority women; costs and benefits of family and work policies; pay equity; wages and employment opportunities; and impact of tax policy on women and families. Specific issues include the impact of the Pregnancy Discrimination Act, pay equity in 20 state civil service systems, and the wage gap between women of color and white women.

Rutgers University, Center for the American Woman and Politics
Eagleton Institute of Politics
New Brunswick, NJ 08901
(908) 932-9384
Dr. Ruth B. Mandel, Director

Research Activities: The nature and extent of women's participation in the U.S., particularly women in state legislatures. Surveys and profiles women candidates and women holding elective or appointive office. Studies impact of women in public office, routes women take into public office, influences on their decision to seek office, and their experiences. Research findings used to recommend specific channels toward office-holding and to encourage more women to enter the electoral process.

Smith College, Project on Women and Social Change
138 Elm Street
Northampton, MA 01063
(413) 585-3591
Dr. Susan C. Bourque, Director

Research Activities: Women, including studies in the areas of health and technology, cross-cultural issues, adult development, public policy, gender, and international development.

Stanford University, Institute for Research on Women and Gender
Serra House, Serra Street
Stanford, CA 94305-8640
(415) 723-1994
Deborah L. Rhode, Director

Research Activities: Women and gender, emphasizing the historical, social, and cultural contexts of the experiences of women, including projects on gender discrimination laws, child care, women's autobiographies, mental health, and work, family, and reproductive issues.

State University of New York at Albany, Center for Women in Government
Draper 310
135 Western Avenue
Albany, NY 12222
(518) 442-3900
Florence Bonner, Director

Research Activities: Brings together unions, women's organizations, advocacy organizations, and government officials to address public sector employment issues of interest to women and minorities, including studies on career ladders, promotion processes, pay equity, and other barriers preventing full participation of women and minorities in public service.

Other areas of study include access to public sector jobs for economically disadvantaged and inner city women.

University of Minnesota, Women, Public Policy, and Development Project
Humphrey Institute of Public Affairs
301-19th Avenue South
Minneapolis, MN 55455
(612) 625-2505
Arvonne Fraser, Director

Research Activities: Research and provision of educational materials on the changing economic roles and responsibility of women, women's organizations, and changes in public policy internationally; leadership by and among women; and follow up to the U.N. Decade of Women. Monitors implementation of the Convention on the Elimination of All Forms of Discrimination Against Women, an international treaty, and examines labor force participation and the economic status of women in the U.S.

University of Texas at Arlington, Women and Work Research and Resource Center
Box 19129
Arlington, TX 76019
(817) 273-3973
LaVerne D. Knezek, Director

Research Activities: Women and work, particularly the interrelationships between work and family, women entrepreneurs and owners of small business, and the effect of on-site child care facilities on employee, family, company, and child. Activities encompass studies of demographic trends and projections, education, reentry of mature women to higher education, and sex equity.

MERIT SYSTEM PRINCIPLES
P.L. 95-454, Title I, Section 2301

1. Recruitment should be from qualified individuals from appropriate sources in an endeavor to achieve a work force from all segments of society, and selection and advancement should be determined solely on the basis of relative ability, knowledge, and skills, after fair and open competition which assures that all receive equal opportunity.

2. All employees and applicants for employment should receive fair and equitable treatment in all aspects of personnel management without regard to political affiliation, race, color, religion, national origin, sex, marital status, age or handicapping condition, and with proper regard for their privacy and constitutional rights.

3. Equal pay should be provided for work for equal value, with appropriate consideration of both national and local rates paid by employers in the private sector, and appropriate incentives and recognition should be provided for excellence in performance.

4. All employees should maintain high standards of integrity, conduct, and concern for the public interest.

5. The Federal work force should be used efficiently and effectively.

6. Employees should be retained on the basis of the adequacy of their performance, inadequate performance should be corrected, and employees should be separated who cannot or will not improve their performance to meet required standards.

7. Employees should be provided effective education and training in cases in which such education and training would result in better organizational and individual performance.

8. Employees should be protected against arbitrary action, personal favoritism, or coercion for partisan political purposes, and prohibited from using their official authority and influence for the purpose of interfering with or affecting the result of an election or a nomination for election.

9. Employees should be protected against reprisal for the lawful disclosure of information which the employee reasonably believes evidences a violation of law, rule or regulation, or mismanagement, a gross waste of funds, an abuse of authority, or a substantial and specific danger to public health or safety.

PROHIBITED PERSONNEL PRACTICES
P.L. 95-454, Title I, Sect. 2302

Any employee who has authority to take, direct others to take, recommend, or approve any personnel action, shall not, with respect to such authority:

1. Discriminate for or against any employee or applicant for employment.

2. Solicit or consider any recommendation or statement, oral or written, with respect to any individual who requests or is under consideration for any personnel action unless such recommendation or statement is based on the personal knowledge or records of the person furnishing it and consists of work performance, ability, aptitude, or general qualifications of such individual, or an evaluation of character, loyalty, or suitability.

3. Coerce the political activity of any person, or take any action against any employee or applicant for employment as a reprisal for the refusal of any person to engage in such political activity.

4. Deceive or willfully obstruct any person with respect to such person's right to compete for employment.

5. Influence any person to withdraw from competition for any position for the purpose of improving or injuring the prospects of any other person for employment.

6. Grant any preference or advantage not authorized by law, rule or regulation to any employee or applicant for employment for the purpose of improving or injuring the prospects of any particular person for employment.

7. Appoint, employ, promote, advance or advocate for appointment, employment, promotion, or advancement, in or to

a civilian position any individual who is a relative of such employee if such position is in the agency in which the employee is serving as a public official or over which the employee exercises jurisdiction or control as such an official.

8. Take or fail to take a personnel action with respect to any employee or applicant for employment as a reprisal for a disclosure of information which the employee or applicant reasonably believes evidences a violation of any law, rule or regulation, or mismanagement, a gross waste of funds, an abuse or authority or a danger to public health and safety.

9. Take or fail to take any personnel action against any employee or applicant for employment as a reprisal for the exercise of any appeal right granted by law, rule or regulation.

10. Discriminate for or against any employee or applicant for employment on the basis of conduct which does not adversely affect the performance of the employee or applicant or the performance of others.

11. Take or fail to take any personnel action if the taking of or failure to take such action violates any law, or regulation concerning the merit system principles.

LANDMARKS FOR WOMEN IN THE FEDERAL SERVICE

1775 Mary Katherine Goddard, the first woman to be employed by the national government, was appointed postmaster of the Baltimore Post Office.

1864 The first statutory recognition of federal employment for women established a maximum salary of $600 a year for women clerk-copyists. At that time, male clerks were being paid $1,200 to $1,800 a year.

1870 Congress passed a law which allowed agency heads to appoint women to higher-level clerkships "at their discretion." Based on interpretation of this law, agencies tended to appoint men only to higher-level jobs for the next 92 years.

1883 The Civil Service Act permitted women to compete in civil service examinations. A woman received the highest score on the first test--but she was the second person to be appointed from the register.

1893 After 10 years under the Civil Service Act, the federal departments in Washington were staffed by 8,377 men and by 3,770 women (31 percent of the Washington workforce). Over the years, the number of female civil servants would fluctuate in response to depressions (decreases) and to wars (increases).

1923 The Classification Act made mandatory the principle of equal pay for equal work.

1961 President Kennedy established the Commission on the Status of Women.

1962 The attorney general declared the 1870 law invalid. (Congress would repeal the law 3 years later.)

1963   The Federal Women's Program was established in response to a recommendation from the President's Commission on the Status of Women.

1967   Executive Order 11375 prohibited sex discrimination in the federal government.

1969   Executive Order 11478 integrated the Federal Women's Program into the overall Equal Employment Opportunity Program.

1971   The restriction on women bearing firearms as federal employees was removed, thereby opening many law enforcement jobs to women.

1974   Leave provisions were changed to allow advancing up to 30 days of sick leave for maternity leave, similar to other leave situations.

1976   Veterans preference for peacetime service was eliminated for all persons who entered the military after October.

1977   Congress repealed apportionment, which required the Civil Service Commission to take into account an applicant's voting residence when ranking applicants for consideration for federal employment.

Excerpted from The Federal Women's Program, *Putting Women in Their Place* (#46).

Index

Abbott, Linda M.C., 81
Abraham, Yohannan T., 419
Abramovitz, Mimi, 198
Ahmed, S., 340
Akabas, Sheila H., 446
Allen, B., 302
Allison, Maria T., 376
American Society for Public Administration, National Capital Area Chapter, 1
Andrew, C., 82
Armor, David J., 377
Aron, Cindy S., 157, 158
Arriola, Elvia R., 220
Arroba, Tanya, 2
Ash, Ronald A., 307
Ayman, Roya., 60
Ballou, Patricia K., 462
Barnes, A. Keith, 311
Barnett, Edith, 221
Baron, James N., 120
Bates, Marsh W., 260
Beck, Ann C., 131
Becraft, Carolyn H., 378
Beilby, W., 120

Bellak, Alvin O., 260
Beller, Andrea H., 262
Bem, Sandra Lipsitz, 366
Benimadhu, Prem P., 159
Bennett-Alexander, Dawn D., 222
Bergmann, Barbara R., 3, 121, 261, 383
Berman, Melissa A., 83
Best, Mary A., 458
Beutell, Nicholas J., 448
Bhatnagar, D., 84
Bianchi, Suzanne M., 172
Biernat, Monica, 447
Blanksby, Margaret, 4
Blau, Francine D., 262
Blessing, Buck, 5
Boesel, Andrew, 359
Bonjean, Charles M., 28, 100, 196
Booker, Sharon, 263
Borjas, G.J., 264
Bowdidge, John S., 419
Bowen, Donald D., 298
Brass, D.J., 299
Bremer, Kamala , 6

Brennan, Eileen M., 7
Brezina, Joan Turek, 323
Brophy, Beth, 223
Brunet, Jean, 68
Buchsbaum, Susan, 429
Burgess, Jane, 59
Burke, Ronald J., 300, 301
Burshardt, S.C., 302
Calise, Angela K., 430
Campbell, Bebe Moore, 402
Campbell, Karen E., 303
Cannings, Kathy, 85, 304
Castille-Ahrens, Angella, 199
Cates, Jo, 224
Chertos, Cynthia, 113
Chester, Nia Lane, 17
Chi, Keon S., 265, 266
Chusmir, Leonard H., 124, 327
Clark-Schock, Karen, 373
Clark, Charles S., 225
Clausen, John A., 403
Cleveland, Ceil, 52
Coderre, C., 82
Cohen, R., 130
Cohen, Lynn Renee, 226
Cohen, Scott A., 347
Col, Jeanne Marie, 86
Colwill, Nina L., 125, 324, 325
Connors, Nancy, 431
Conway, Deborah, 456
Cook, Alice H., 420
Cooley, Cathy A., 432
Cooper, Cary, 8, 449
Cooper, Elizabeth A., 284
Coppolino, Yolanda, 53
Corder, Judy A., 28, 100, 196

Cote-O'Hara, Jocelyn, 87
Coyle, A., 132
Crawford, J.D., 379
Crosby, F., 200
Crouse, Janice Shaw, 305
Cullen, D., 88
Daley, Dennis M., 326
Darwent, Charles, 306
David, Marilyn H., 227
Davidson, Marilyn J., 8, 449
Davis, Mari, 463
Denis, A., 82
Desai, Sonalde, 404
DeVries, Christine M., 133
Diener, Thomas, 360
Dinitto, D., 102
Dipboye, R.L., 89
DiPrete, Thomas A., 9, 10, 134, 192
Dixon, Penelope, 464
Doherty, Kathleen, 421
Dometrius, Nelson C., 160
Dreher, George F., 307
Drygulski, Barbara Wright, ed., 69
Dubno, Peter, 201
Duerst Lahti, Georgia, 54
Duncan, Margaret C., 376
Duncan, Emily, 380
Durand, Douglas E., 124, 327
Durant, Jr., Lucius, 477
Edmonds, Jean, 87
Ehrenreich, Nancy S., 228
Ehrensaft, Diane, 405
Ehrhart, Julie Kahn, 381
Ehrlich, E., 406

Index

Ely, John Hart, 229
Emmert, Mark A., 276
England, Robert E., 247
Epstein, C., 126
Estrich, Susan, 230
Evans, Sara M., 267
Fagenson, Ellen A., 135, 308
Falkenberg, L., 382
Faludi, Susan, 202
Farley, Jennie, 407
Fasman, Zachary, 161
Federally Employed Women, 90, 231, 433
Ferguson, K.E., 136
Field, Susan, 434
Fields, Daisy B., 11
Figart, Deborah M., 12, 383
Filene, Peter J., 328
Fine, Marlene G., 329
Fisher, Anne B., 384
Fitzgerald, Patricia A., 361
Flammang, Janet A., 268
Forbes, J. Benjamin, 13, 91
Forsythe, Sandra M., 330
Fraker, S., 92
Fraser, Jill A., 14
Freeman, Sue J.M., 70
Friedman, D.E., 93, 422
Fritchie, R., 129
Fritz, Norma R., 232
Galagan, Patricia., 15
Gerhart, Barry., 269
Giannantonio, Christina M., 372
Gibbs, Nancy, 233
Gibish, Jane E., 465
Ginorio, Angela, 250
Glasner, Daniel M., 260
Gluck, Sherna Berger, 385

Gold, Una O., 331
Goldman, Nancy Loring, 386
Goldsmith, Elizabeth B., 408
Green, Lisa Naparstek, 203
Greene, Pamela, 387
Greene, Robert J., 270
Greenhaus, Jeffrey H., 16
Gregory, A., 55
Grossman, Hildreth Y., 17
Guerin, Cecily, 319
Guinn, Stephen L., 71
Gutek, Barbara A., 18, 122, 234
Ha, Meesung, 99
Haignere, Lois, 113
Halas, Cecelia, 332
Hale, Mary M., 59, 162, 193
Hall, Holly, 450
Hall, Douglas T., 409
Hammond, Valerie, 362
Handley, Elisabeth A., 56
Hardesty, Sarah, 94
Harlan, Sharon L., 363, 390
Harriman, Ann, 333
Harris, Diane, 435
Harrison, D., 102
Hartman, Bruce W., 334
Hartmann, H., 123
Harvey, Carol, 19
Hauck, Vern E., 235
Haw, Mary A., 451
Hearn, Jeff, 57
Heilman, M.E., 137, 204-206
Hemmelgarn, Brenda, 452
Henning, M., 20
Herchenroether, Sherry, 436
Herlihy, J.M., 137
Hill, M. Anne, 272

Hill, John P., 411
Hitt, Michael A., 455
Hodgson, Richard C., 354
Hojat, Mohammadreza, 423
Hollenbeck, John R., 335
Horn, Gregory, 311
Horner, Constance, 273
Howard, Rosemary E., 309
Howe, Deborah A., 6
Howell, Ruth S., 364
Hoy, Judith, 365
Hurley, Charlotte, 479
Hurst, Marsha, 466
Hyworon, Zorianna L., 80
Ilgen, Daniel R., 335
Jacobs, Nehama, 94
Jacobs, Daniel J., 467
Jacobson, Aileen, 21
Jaiprakash, Indira, 336
James, Kim, 2
James, Chuck, 95
Jardin, A., 20
Jennings, Daniel F., 410
Johansen, Elaine, 274
Johnson, Fern L., 329
Johnson, A., 127
Johnston, William B., 72
Joice, Wendell H., 437
Jorgensen, Mary Anne, 468
Jost, Kenneth, 163
Kahn, Alfred J., 73
Kamerman, Sheila, 73
Kandel, William L., 236
Kanter, Rosabeth Moss, 96, 97
Kantrowitz, Barbara, 237
Katz, D., 207
Kaufman, Leslie., 238

Kay, Susan Ann, 164
Kazemek, Edward A., 58
Kellough, J. Edward, 164-167
Kelly, Rita Mae, 22, 59, 162
Kennedy, Susan Estabrook, 469
Kennedy, R. Bryan, 98
Killingsworth, Mark R., 272
Kingsley, J. Donald, 138
Kirk, Delaney J., 246
Kitfield, James, 388
Kleiner, Brian H., 107
Koman, Joseph J., 411
Korabik, Karen, 60
Kraft, Joan F., 74
Kranz, Harry, 139
Krislov, Samuel, 140, 141
LaFleur, Elizabeth K., 424
Laing, Gail, 452
Larwood, Laurie, 18
Lasky, Barbara, 374
Leavitt, Judith A., 470-472
Lee, R.A., 23
Levine, Charles H., 75
Lewis, Chad T., 275
Lewis, Gregory B., 25, 26, 94,
    99, 168, 194, 209,
    276, 277, 337-339
Lewittes, Hedva J., 366
Light, Nancy, 210
Lincoln, J.R., 312
Linenberger, Patricia, 239
Little, Danity M., 24
Lombardo, Michael M., 367
London, Manuel, 27
Lovrich, Nicholas, 287
Luna, Gaye, 278
Luneburg, William V., 142

Index

Macken, Patrick O., 100
Mainiero, Lisa A., 110
Mangum, Stephen L., 279
Mann, M., 280
Marie, Cathy, 54
Markham, William T., 28, 29, 100, 196
Marshall, J., 31
Martell, R.F., 204, 206
Martin, P., 102
Martin, Lynn, 101
Matthews, Michael D., 459
Mauksch, Hans O., 213
Maupin, Rebekah J., 61
McBride, Angela B., 453
McBroom, Patricia A., 30
McCaghy, M. Dawn, 473
McCall, Morgan W., 367
McCaney, M., 340
McClellan, Elizabeth, 348
McCullough, Rita J., 474
McEnrue, M.P., 195
McFeely, Mary Drake, 475
McGlen, N. E., 281
McKeen, Carol A., 300, 301
McKenzie, Edna, 87
McPherson, J.A., 310
Meier, Sara Beth, 240
Meier, Kenneth J., 143, 144
Mendelson, Jack L., 311
Mendenhall, Janice, 169
Mendez, Carmen, 345
Metcalfe, B.P., 341
Michelson, William, 425
Miller, J., 312
Miller, Angela B., 454
Miller, Eleanor M., 213
Moesel, Doug, 455

Montmarquette, Claude, 304
Moore, L.L., ed., 103
Moore, Kris K., 45, 352
Morehead, Joe, 241
Morlacci, Maria, 242
Morphet, Janice, 32
Morrison, Ann M., 62, 104, 367
Moss, Peter, 426
Munch, Joan S., 309
Murray, P.J., 243
Nachmias, David, 33, 145
National Council for Research on Women, 476
Nelson, Barbara J., 267
Nelson, Debra L., 455
Nelton, Sharon, 63
Newell, Terry, 368
Newland, Chester A., 369
Newsom, Walter B., 424
Nodell, Bobbi, 105
Noe, Raymond A., 313
O'Connor, K., 281
O'Donnell, Holly, 355
O'Farrell, Brigid, 390
O'Hare, Marianne M., 448
Olson, J., 312
Orr, Elaine L., 438
Ospina, Sonia, 106
Ostroff, Cheri, 335
Owens, Otis Holloway, 360
Paddison, Lorraine, 434
Park, Kyungho, 339
Parks, Gregory, 34
Parlee, Mary Brown, 356
Paton, A., 146
Paul, N., 314
Paulson, Sharon E., 411

Pave, Irene, 342
Pazy, Asya, 315
Pearce, Thomas G., 235
Pearson, Dick, 128
Peder, M., 129
Pell, Arthur R., 38
Peters, Lawrence H., et. al., 211
Piatz, Brenda, 391
Pickering, Tonya H., 107
Piercy, James E., 13
Piper, J., 23
Pitcher, Fiona, 64
Podmore, D., 396
Posner, Barry Z., 35
Poston, Ersa H., 36
Povall, M., 108
Powell, Gary N., 245, 343, 344
Powell, James D., 246
President's Commission on the Status of Women, 147
Pringle, Judith K., 331
Proulx, Serge, 68
Pulliam, L. Lynne, 427
Purcell, Deborah Ross, 170
Quick, James C., 455
Ragins, Belle Rose, 316
Ralson, David A., 439
Redclift, Nanneke, 109
Rehfuss, John A., 171
Reich, Murray H., 317
Reinhardt, Denise, 212
Remick, Helen, 250, 282, 283
Repper, D.P., 205
Reskin, Barbara F., 123, 392
Rexford, Stephen J., 110
Riccucci, Norma M., 37

Richter, Werner, 76
Rizzo, Ann-Marie, 345
Robinson, Robert K., 246
Rogalin, Wilma C., 38
Roos, Patricia A., 392, 412
Rosenberg, Sheila, 346
Rosenbloom, David H., 141, 145, 148
Rosener, Judy B., 65
Rosenfeld, Rachel A., 42
Rosenzweig, Julie M., 7
Ross, Cynthia S., 247
Ruble, T., 130
Ruble, D., 130
Rumberger, Russell W., 39
Ryan, M. Sallyanne, 329
Rytina, Nancy F., 172
Salibury, Jan, 250
Sanders, Jo Shuchat, 393
Sandler, Bernice R., 381
Sargeant, Alice, 66
Saurage, J.G., 216
Scarr, Sandra, 428
Scheibal, William, 285
Schmidt, Warren H., 35
Schmitt, Neal, 347
Schneider, Barbara Ann, 456
Scholl, Richard W., 284
Schroeder, Patricia, 273
Schwartz, Helen, 364
Schwartz, Felice N., 413
Scott, Karen R., 40
Scott, K. Dow, 348
Seath, Carol B., 53
Sharma, Sarla, 67
Shea David J., 377
Sheldon, Roger A., 41

Sheldon, Suzanne E., 41
Sherwood, Diane, 394
Shukla, Archana, 457
Shukra, Nidhi, 457
Siegenthaler, Jurg K., 74
Sigelman, Lee, 149
Simon, M.C., 205, 206
Sinclair, Thea M., 109
Slack, James D., 187
Smeltzer, L.R., 358
Smith, Emily, 395
Smith, Kathleen A., 248
Solomon, Charlene Marmer, 111
Sorenson, Elaine, 286
Soule, Whitman T., 134, 192
South, Scott J., 28, 196, 349
Spann, Jeri, 249
Spencer, A., 396
Spenner, Kenneth I., 42
Spruell, G., 112
Stamp, Gillian, 43
Stark, Elizabeth, 370
Statham, Anne, 213
Stead, B.A., 44
Steel, Brent S., 197, 287
Steinberg, Ronnie, 113, 363
Stern, Barbara B., 318
Stevens, Cynthia Kay, 275
Still, Leonie V., 319
Stivers, Camilla, 350
Stohr-Gillmore, Mary K., 131
Strauss, Marcy, 214
Stringer, Donna M., 250
Stumpf, Stephen A., 27
Suojanen, Waino W., 351
Sussal, Carol M., 320

Sutton, Charlotte Decker, 45, 352
Sylvester, Kathleen, 288
Tannen, Deborah, 357
Tanner, Lucretia Dewey, 323
Task Force on Barriers to Women in the Public Service, 114
Taylor, Patricia A., 371
Taylor, M. Susan, 372
Tell, David, 150
Terpstra, David E., 251
The Bureau of National Affairs, 401
Trenk, Barbara Scherr, 414
Turner, Yolanda, 373
Turner, David A., 369
United States Congress. House. Committee on Armed Services. Military Personnel and Compensation Subcommittee, 397
United States Congress. House. Committee on Education and Labor. Subcommittee on Employment Opportunities, 151
United States Congress. House. Committee on Foreign Affairs, 174, 176
United States Congress. House. Committee on Post Office and Civil Service. Subcommittee

on Investigations, 254
United States Congress.
Senate. Committee on Labor,
398
U.S. Bureau of Mines, 252
U.S. Civil Service
Commission.
Manpower Statistics
Division, 173, 174
U.S. Commission on Civil
Rights, 216, 253
U.S. Department of the
Interior, 152
U.S. Department of Labor
Women's Bureau, 399
U.S. General Accounting
Office, 115, 116, 153,
178-183, 188, 189,
289, 415
U.S. Merit Systems Protection
Board, 117, 440, 255,
256
U.S. Office of Personnel
Management, 46, 47,
77, 184, 290, 416,
417
U.S. Office of Personnel
Management. Office
of Affirmative
Employment
Programs, 190, 191
U.S. Office of Personnel
Management.
Personnel Systems and
Oversight Group, 175
U.S. Office of Personnel
Management.
Supervisory and
Communications
Training Center, 257
Van Fleet, D. D., 216
Van Velsor, Ellen, 62, 104
Vancouver, Jeffrey B., 335
Vaughan, Edward, 374
Verespej, Michael A., 441
Vertz, Laura L., 118, 154,
291
Voydanoff, Patricia, 418
Waite, Linda J., 404
Walker, Lorraine O., 458
Ward, T., 48
Warner, Rebecca L., 197
Washington Council of
Lawyers, 155
Watkins, Kathleen Pullan, 477
Watson, Eileen D., 354
Watson, Camilla E., 215
Weaver, Charles N., 459
Webster, George D., 292
Weiss, Rhoda, 321
Werbel, J.D., 358
Werwie, Doris M., 293
Wesman, Elizabeth C., 294
Wester, Jennifer, 78
White, Randall P., 62, 104
Wilds, Nancy G., 258
Wilkinson, Carroll Wetzel,
478
Willborn, Steven, 295
Wilson, Guy, 479
Wilson, John W., 460
Winebrenner, Hugh, 296
Wise, Lois Recascino, 297
Witt, L. Alan, 460

Wolf, Dona, 375
Wong, Lisa M. L., 461
Wooldridge, Blue, 78
Wortman, Camille B., 447
Wright, Ruth, 159
Wright, Barbara Drygulski, 79
Wurster, Barbara C., 156
Yoder, Janice D., 186
Zambrana, Ruth, 466